# Where Do The Children Play?

*Funding for this Study Guide was provided by*

Ruth Mott Foundation

# Where Do The Children Play?

## A Study Guide to the Film

EDITED BY **Elizabeth Goodenough**

*Designed by Jody Fisher and David Lindsey, Ann Arbor, Michigan*

*Photographs by Jody Fisher unless otherwise noted*

*Cover design and photograph by Jody Fisher*

*Back cover photograph by Mark Powell*

MICHIGAN TELEVISION
WFUM TV-28
michigantelevision.org

*for Will, Jamie, and Gil*
*where it all began*

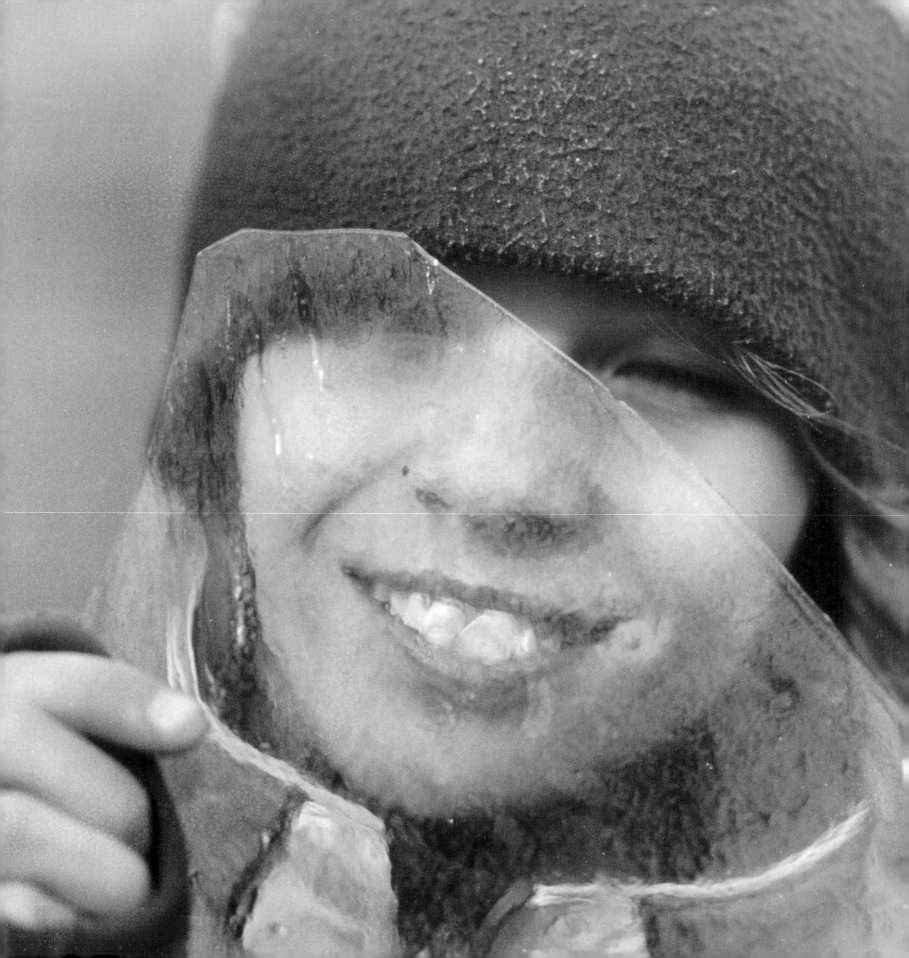

**Elizabeth Goodenough**

# ACKNOWLEDGMENTS

On the long pilgrimage toward the achievement of a documentary film, there must be many believers. Five years ago the offices of University of Michigan Interim President Joseph White and Senior Vice Provost Lester Monts provided seed funding for this project. When Michigan Television later agreed to take on the production of the film developed originally in collaboration with Christopher Cook and Katherine Weider, Jay Nelson and Jennifer Howard of Michigan Public Media and Maureen Martin worked to develop further and define outreach and film components. Grants from the Ruth Mott Foundation for Flint outreach, the film and this Study Guide launched "Where Do the Children Play?" Further grants from The W. K. Kellogg Foundation and Blue Cross/Blue Shield of Michigan enabled us to arrive at our destination: to begin making a film.

Along the way Sheila Wilder, Melanie Karner, Craig Regester and Charlie Bright of the Residential College at the University of Michigan supported fundraising and outreach efforts, while RC students provided inspiration, initiative and industry in development of this volume. Malika Middlebrooks who helped with this Study Guide and Ayn Reineke, Nithya Joseph, and Alex Gorsuch photographed by David Lamb on the title page of the Children's Portfolio represent the finest artistic talent that Residential College students bring to projects such as this one. Subjects for the film were selected from among school children they met through their fieldwork in the course called The Poetry of Everyday Life, which Fred Peters of the Literature Program enabled me to teach. I want to thank Julie Ellison of the University of Michigan for her early model of this course and Matt Perry and Rosemarie Hester for their intelligence and flair in devising models of collaboration for my college students and their fourth and fifth graders at Ann Arbor Academy and Summers-Knoll School. Robert Grese of the Nichols Arboretum and Matthaei Botanical Gardens welcomed us to use his beautiful outdoor facilities for class meetings. Laurence Goldstein, editor of the *Michigan Quarterly Review*, provided such faith in the Secret Spaces of Childhood and the double issue of *MQR* that he devoted to this subject that others came to see the cause as worthy. The book *Secret Spaces of Childhood* published by the University of Michigan provided the bedrock for this project thanks to Phil Pochoda and Mary Bisbee-Beek.

Working with gifted fundraisers and generous funders was made possible by Susan Howbert from the Council of Michigan Foundations who proved to be an angel of wisdom with her advice, tenacity and counsel. Leslie Lee and the Herrington-Fitch Family Foundation provided funding as well as hospitality and inspiration in the earth-centered retreat of Pine Hollow for pilgrims along the way: Betsy Upton Stover, Nancy Colina, Carol Payne McGovern, and Susan Glass. All of these individuals and family foundations cherish the ideal of outdoor play and universal access to natural spaces for all children.

From these special relationships came grants from the Colina Foundation, the DeRoy Testamentary Foundation, and the R. E. Olds Foundation. Sally and Ian Bund provided funding as well as the best that friendship offers: ongoing enthusiasm, gatherings of support, vital conversations. Lana Pollack of the Michigan Environmental Council, Rob Collier of the Council of Michigan Foundations, Joan Almon of the Alliance for Childhood and Lisa Wozniak of the Michigan League of Conservation Voters understood the difficulties and supported the importance of the project. For expanding outreach, including this Study Guide and an edited anthology on play to be published in 2008, I am grateful to Annie Martin of Wayne State University Press Landscapes of Childhood series. Miguel Satut of the W. K. Kellogg Foundation enabled Roundtable, Inc. to launch a national engagement campaign under the enlightened leadership of Martha Fowlkes and Robert Lavelle (whose campaign strategy appears in these pages). Friends like Peggy Ellsberg, Stuart Brown, Percy Bates, Rebecca McGowan, Jeanne Hinte-Levy, Margaret Butler and my mother Margaret van Dusen helped me know I was not walking alone. For friends who gave time and thought, I want to thank Jan Cohen and Jody Fisher who gave unstintingly. Without their help I could not have completed this book.

# Contents

*Fairy & troll houses should look so natural that they are almost hidden. A location close to the ground is best, and a clearly defined path leading to the house helps fairies and trolls find their way.*

*Use only natural materials. Dry grasses, leaves, sticks, pebbles and pinecones are just a few examples of materials to choose.*

*Be careful not to use or disturb any of nature's materials that are still living, especially flowers, ferns, mosses and lichen. Fairies & trolls like to protect anything that is growing in nature.*

FAIRY & TROLL HOUSE BUILDING GUIDELINES

(ADAPTED FROM WWW.FAIRYHOUSES.COM)

**Elizabeth Goodenough**

# INTRODUCTION

## Beginning with Play

*To see a World in a Grain of Sand*
*And a Heaven in a Wild Flower*
*Hold Infinity in the palm of your hand*
*And Eternity in an hour*

WILLIAM BLAKE, *AUGURIES OF INNOCENCE* (1863)

Born and raised in southeastern Michigan, I loved our State Mitten. My own fingers and palms, straight up and sideways, held a map of upper and lower peninsulas. To a child, this manual geography made perfect sense: standing each morning to pledge allegiance to the flag, we in Michigan were the two hands at the heart of our country.

In school we sang, "Take a trip to Michigan, in a boat or car or plane or train, and you will find that Michigan is the place you want to see again," a burst of musical chauvinism I connected with the 1954 Water Wonderland license plate, the 1960s Great Lakes State and our slogan supreme: Water-Winter Wonderland.

When I moved to Boston in 1970 to enroll in Harvard graduate school specializing in Victorian literature, I was inwardly drawn back to the places where I'd grown up: the pine woods behind our house, Lake Huron in the summer, our flat, graveled rooftop. What I loved most about these locales made no natural arc to the work I was doing until I wrote my dissertation on Virginia Woolf. There I found children playing like gods. Building a sand castle, capturing a crab, cutting out a picture, they embodied moments of creative authority and inexpressible delight. Adults, I discovered in her novels, become routinely articulate only to lose curiosity or to forget such simple thrills.

To understand Woolf's romantic pessimism, and the excitement of play and place in her novels, I researched books from her youth: not just the Victorians Leslie Stephen read to his children such as Hawthorne and Dickens but also texts like *Robinson Crusoe*, *Alice's Adventures in Wonderland*, and *Peter Pan and Wendy*. I developed a taste for crossing the bridge between juvenile classics and highbrow prose for adults, finding links among books for and about children such as *The Adventures of Huckleberry Finn*, *The Secret Garden* and the Narnia series in unusual literary locales. I noticed that more than any episode or character, an unforgettable place at the heart of the child-centered stories radiated the meaning of the whole. Each world apart expressed complete fulfillment yet eluded plot summary.

Somehow the child figure and idyllic space merge in an utterly new way of seeing and becoming. Regardless of size or scale, Huck's raft,

Avery's barn, and Pooh's Hundred Acre Wood offer escape and "emotional survival," as Brian Sutton-Smith defines play in his forthcoming book. William Blake, the first English picture book artist who engraved and water colored each *Songs of Innocence and Experience* by hand, capitalized Imagination. For him Vision is divine: perception of auguries in the everyday, creation of voice and self. His words take root in the ground, but they dance up like flames.

The purpose of this volume is to enable children and adults, together and alone, to recapture energy, joy and insight in moments like those on Blake's echoing green or Woolf's seashore through play, storytelling and the arts. For grown-ups, this Study Guide might lead to Roald Dahl's mantra: get down on your knees for a week to recall what it's like "when the people with power literally loom over you" (Talbot 2005, 94). For children, it may affirm their own originality and scope, whether making hideouts or forts, doing puppetry or performing, finding some all-for-me space or magic circle where they're at the center. Up a tree or under a bed, a self-ish place may be close to home and quite small, but it's freely chosen and a perfect fit.

A companion to the film "Where Do the Children Play?" this volume grows from a collaboration between Christopher Cook's award-winning documentary "The Sprawling of America" and my *Secret Spaces of Childhood* (University of Michigan Press, 2003). Three-time Oscar-winner Mark Harris was invited to become consulting producer because his "Redwoods" and "Into the Arms of Strangers" focused on forests and childhood, subjects not easily represented on screen. The challenge of capturing the voice and awareness of the young is well described by Christopher Cook in "Making a Documentary Film" and by Jeff Kupperman who invited high school students to help fourth and fifth graders produce their own documentaries.

Although societies tend to identify children and nature as property rather than as process (in Blake's auguries a cosmic interdependence), we are patterned in ways that define us later on, as producer Jennifer White recalls in the smell of homegrown tomatoes. The curiosity, observation, and engagement we bring to our first environments are transferred to every landscape of endeavor that follows whether in business, science or the arts. Joe L. Frost's summary of how childhood play underlies human history combines discussion of that evolutionary continuum with its transformation in recent decades.

Using our vanished frontier as a marker of Americans' relationship to nature, Richard Louv, author of *Last Child in the Woods: Saving our Children from Nature-Deficit Disorder*, sets the stage for understanding that children themselves have become our last frontier. Their bodies, minds and spirits are now contested ground in our changing global order. Choices made by planning and school boards, parks and corpora-tions, families and legislators today will determine how the next generation envisions the future and reshapes the earth. The Improvisation Across Fields seminars developing at the University of Michigan remind me that Froebel's open-ended blocks, discussed by Mary Ruth Moore, shaped the kindergarten movement and symbolic play for almost two centuries.

A time machine such as Jeanne Schinto imagines in her essay on the Bruce Museum can take us back to natural and man-made landscapes—Western ghost towns, the Huron River or a mall—that have profoundly shaped the way we Americans see our selves and our society. But "if children ruled the world," as Claire Gallagher suggests, more nature and animals might be embedded in urban design as metaphors for the cycle of life and experiences within it.

Creativity develops through exploration, storytelling, and secret world building. Engaging the local is a child's work and play, the only way personal domains are enlarged. Certainly this process of self-discovery deserves to be treated with as much care by educators and families as the cultivation of literacy and the mastery of mathematical skills in schools. Yet we know little, it seems, about the intersection between play and the inspiration recreation draws from its physical context.

A pioneer in such research, Roger Hart of the Children's Environments Research Group, has studied children over three decades in a New

England town and New York City. Looking at the suburban, urban and rural continuum, he finds in "Where Do the Children Play?" many of the questions the nation is beginning to ask about play in relation to obesity and children's informal learning about the natural world: "it goes well beyond these two important issues to deal more broadly with how children's free time has changed. It challenges communities of all kinds to address the policy issues that need to be faced in relation to children's outdoor activities and their health and well-being."

One of those most important issues considered in section III is how wildlands, adventure playgrounds and play workers might overcome exclusion and isolation so that children of all abilities have access to play and natural resources. Zoning that permits sprawl, prohibits sidewalks, and isolates housing from recreational areas forces adults to drive children to parks and playgrounds. Disabled children, arguably, face the greatest barriers to outdoor play. If the local playground is accessible by ramp and curb cut, the equipment often is not. Yet Penny Wilson shows how inclusive play can enhance the liveliness and fun of everybody.

Playgrounds provide a microcosmic peek at the culture of their designers. True adventure playgrounds, Catherine Davis states, "are impossible in the US due to insurance and litigation." Having designed and built an adventure playground and attached building using recycled materials over a period of four years as an architecture student in London, Davis could not transplant her "Crumbles Playground." But in a democratic society, different combinations and forms of adventure playgrounds might evolve incorporating gross motor challenges, construction of rough-built housing by younger or older children, habitats for rabbits, an owl or a goat. Inventive throwbacks and cross-fertilizations remain possible. Jean Vortkamp's Front Porch, a homegrown settlement house, turns a Detroit neighborhood into close-knit community. In Roger Hart's 1982 description of wildlands, I see the roots of Wild Zones, now being seeded around the world by the British David Hawkins, founding Project Manager of The Edible Schoolyard in Berkeley, California. Sponsored in this country by the Alliance for Childhood, British playworker Penny Wilson works with staff at Franklin Park outside Chicago.

Jane Jacobs in *The Life and Death of Great American Cities* (1961) notes that "social capital" in urban areas accrues when planners promote informal contact among neighbors: street crime lessens, children are happier and better cared for. Levels of social trust are raised when walk to school programs succeed, as Hugh McDiarmid's photo essay shows in Detroit, a city with its share of vandalism, graffiti, and the "epidemic of violence" that Barack Obama sees "sickening the soul of this nation." Yet in our most devastated neighborhoods, where safety issues force children to stay inside, after school programs such as Bart Hirsch details also thrive. Ann Arbor may falter in a walk to school initiative, but its Neutral Zone welcomes a quirky ecology of teenage peer groups in control of public space as Mark Stranahan and Jacoby Simmons indicate. It takes tremendous civic will and anti-crime efforts beginning at home to counteract the killing occurring in rundown schoolyards.

During school, unstructured, open-ended play is essential to the health of the young. As Vejoya Viren reports in these pages, it enhances social skills, teaches conflict resolution increases fitness, improves learning and reduces stress by connecting youth with natural environments. Aggressive argument, pushing and shoving, and other forms of pecking order conflict, particularly amongst boys, often lead to elimination of recess. Teachers in K-8 grades are quick to read conflict as an automatic disqualifier of free group play. A younger generation of teachers who have not experienced recess themselves may sacrifice undirected play in an attempt to provide a self-contradiction—the "risk-free playground," to sanitize legitimate adventure, or to implement the "Trouble-Free Playground." Even bullying, conflict that exceeds reasonable boundaries, is often cited as a rationale for getting rid of recess, yet it too can provide for learning as well as teaching moments. Stacey Coates, author of articles and pamphlets on violence prevention, cooperative learning, and on team building, con-

ducts workshops using drama to achieve curricular objectives as well as to address intolerance. Many Friends (Quaker) schools empower children to resolve group conflicts through faculty training and student instruction that begins in pre-school.

Although playgrounds themselves often become the most contentious sites for school administrators, Clements and Svane make me wonder why community organizing does not aim at making schoolyards the most beautiful, green, and alive places in the neighborhood. Such locales could provide the moral and aesthetic cohesion that Holmes School offers in the film. Hamady Elementary in Flint welcomes playworker Penny Wilson to its classrooms, and my Residential College students from the University of Michigan team up with elementary school pupils on trips to a dam, arboretum and cemetery. On field trips I began to understand that college students can act as god-like human beings to a child. Going down the railroad tracks, younger and older youth find "treasure": bottle caps, plastic containers, broken jewelry. A piece of ice becomes a nature-stained glass window photographed by RC student David Lamb on page vi. A hubcap is likewise transformed into a work of art through the synergy of these partners. The poetry and images of the Children's Portfolio: "The World is Round So Let It Spin" reveal that the college students were as liberated by bushwhacking and getting wet and dirty as were the fourth and fifth graders. Their teacher, Rosemarie Hester, gave us "all the equipment to go on the safari of the mind."

Communities, teachers, and families need to organize a resistance movement against the rigid all-day confinement of children in schools. In their essays, Ed Miller, Diane Levin, and Susan Linn offer practical suggestions and key reforms in and out of school. They argue for environments away from television, computers, graphically violent video games, microchip embedded toys and "the loud voice of commerce." There's a cost to children's inability to have a private life in nature and to explore on their own with peers or animals and to enjoy that freedom.

"Sometimes generations reverse their patterns and that's what I'm hoping will happen here, that by talking about play, by sharing play, by activating play these young people will begin to see what they missed and they'll make sure that their children have it, because they'll see how vital it is," Joan Almon says at the end of the film. My hope is that a successful national engagement campaign outlined by Robert Lavelle spurs such a reversal, but that adult intrusion on childhood is minimal. How best to master this precarious balance—ensuring but not controlling the rights of all children to gain access to outdoor recreation? First, we must invest as citizens, families, and neighbors in semi-wild and safe locales that ensure holistic connection with nature. Nurturing natural resources for future generations avoids "adulteration" of play and colonizing our own children. Secondly, we need to connect more deeply with ourselves. Martha Travers, Jan Drucker, Loranne Carbon, and Nancy Wolfe offer ways to follow this path.

Finally, we must recognize the tension between generations and enjoy the unexpected when it happens as a force of nature, as Jonathan Fairbanks does on a family reunion. In special conversation or celebration such as Ellen Handler Spitz, Sharon Schneider, Joyce Hemphill and Cindy Dell Clark describe, "reality glitters." With this phrase of Thylias Moss to guide us, may we be free enough to be simple, to follow the spiritual wisdom offered by Penny Wilson: "You know, just let the children play. Go out and sit and watch. They'll be fine. Just trust to it."

### Notes
Talbot, Margaret. 2005. *The Candy Man: Why Children Love Roald Dahl's Stories—and Why Many Adults Don't.* The New Yorker 81, no. 2:92

For a long time I have considered children's secret hideaways to be a fundamental trait of human nature. The tendency to build them is, I believe, one of the epigenetic rules that compose human nature—a hereditary regularity in mental development that predisposes us to acquire certain preferences and to undertake practices of ultimate value in survival. From the secret places come an identification with place, a nourishing of individuality and self-esteem, and an enhanced joy in the construction of habitation. They also bring us close to the earth and nature, in ways that can ensure a lifelong love of both.

EDWARD O. WILSON
SECRET SPACES OF CHILDHOOD

**Making a Documentary Film**

# Jennifer White

When I was growing up in Detroit, most of my time was spent outdoors. There were dozens of remarkable nooks in my crowded neighborhood; you just had to take the time to find them. My favorite place was a plot of ground, about three feet across, which ran between the side of our house and our neighbor's backyard fence. My mother grew tomatoes in that small strip during the summer months. She'd send me back to pick them and, though I was not a fan of tomatoes, I relished the time I spent there, testing for ripeness, enjoying the feel of the soil and inhaling the distinctive scent of tomatoes on the vine.

My parents have since moved out of the city and now have a house on an acre of land in a quiet corner of Southfield, Michigan. Their garden is much larger now, and the tomatoes are no longer contained to a small strip of land beside the house. My niece, a precocious toddler, will gleefully climb into the tomato patch, squish her toes in the dirt and eat the ripened fruit directly from the vine. She'll pluck a cherry tomato and hold it as close to her eye as she can, searching for some detail known only to her. She'll hold the tomato out to me gasping, "Oh my!" Then she'll pop the tomato in her mouth, enjoying the burst of the fruit in her mouth. She'll repeat this ritual until her tummy and shirt are full of ripe toma-

> **"Then she'll pop the tomato in her mouth, enjoying the burst of the fruit in her mouth."**

to juice. Something happens in those moments, something very similar to my experience as a child. There is a cadence, an order to life that we discover. This is the ground, this grows from the ground, I can pick this, I can eat this, this is the ground, this grows from the ground, I can pick this, I can eat this. Each summer this cycle repeats itself and even if tomatoes don't hold the same wonder at 13 or 30 years of age, that cadence is renewed when I discover vine ripened tomatoes at the grocery store. That scent of earth and sun still clings to them and, even now, I hold them to my nose and remember that tiny strip of earth behind our house.

The outdoors holds hundreds, if not thousands of these cadences, waiting to be discovered. I worry what happens to them if they stop being discovered, if the rhythms found in nature are completely replaced by the hum of electronics. The documentary "Where Do the Children Play?" examines this issue and also gives us a glimpse into the worlds of children for whom nature is still a wonder.

**Jennifer White, station manager of Michigan Television, a service of Michigan Public Media, is executive producer of "Where Do the Children Play?"**

# Christopher Cook

When we finally got into production with "Where Do The Children Play?" in the spring of 2006, I knew that it would be a tough film to make because interviewing children can be very tricky. I just never knew how much.

For months through the summer and into the fall, it seemed as though we would go from one interview to the next without ever getting a good sound bite. "Yes" and "no" answers do not make a movie. But then we would suddenly hit a little gold mine of articulation, like Jewell Gillespie, the boy in the Beaver Island section of the film. Or Alec, in the section on suburbs, who likes the indoors because "that's where the computers are." Or, the Eyster children—Artemis, Harold and Ted—who open and close the film and whose connection to nature and self-assuredness is breathtaking.

I came to their interviews a doubter about home schooling, and left with a deep appreciation that it works well when it is outfitted with strong preparation and careful choices of when a child will be launched and integrated into the full public school system.

Overall, "Where Do The Children Play?" is one of the most difficult films I have worked on.

Films are basically stories. And when stories come together, I find, there is not much to do but follow them. They take on a life of their own and point the way. I have made more than 20 hours of documentary film in the last eight years and each, except this one, told itself on paper for me before we ever began editing.

But "Where Do They Children Play?" fought me every step of the way. So much so that I would write a section without any real idea of how it really sounded or how the whole film would hang together. Then I'd ask Matt Zacharias, the editor, to "string it out" on the screen so that I could hear and see it, and then change it again. It wasn't until it was on the screen that the film began to gel for me.

"Where Do The Children Play?" will occupy a special place in my experience as a filmmaker. It taught me that there are many ways, other than my preferred route, to make a film.

> **"And when stories come together, I find, there is not much to do but follow them."**

**Christopher Cook is an EMMY-award winning producer, director, and writer who lives in Ann Arbor, Michigan. His documentary work has appeared on regional public television, commercial television stations, and cable stations such as History Channel. Since 1997, he has researched, written, produced, and directed more than 14 hours of documentary programming, most of which has appeared on regional PBS stations, for which he has received eleven EMMYs. Cook produced and wrote documentary programs from 1999-2007 for Michigan Public Television's "Michigan at Risk" series, four of which won EMMYs. Other EMMYs included "Sprawling of America," one of three nominees for best limited series in the International Documentary Association Awards in 2002.**

# Mark Harris

As someone who grew up with a forest for a backyard, I felt an immediate affinity for the subject matter of this film. When I was 13, the bulldozers razed the woods I had played in as a child in Scranton, Pennsylvania, to build Park Gardens, a series of squat, brick apartment houses whose only aspirations of beauty were its name.

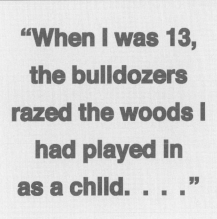

"When I was 13, the bulldozers razed the woods I had played in as a child. . . ."

My parents immediately built a fence and planted trees to block out this new suburban blight, but for me their efforts only emphasized what I had lost. My world had narrowed, shrunk. The freedom I had had to hunt for snakes and frogs, to climb a tree and nestle with a book in its branches, or just sit there with only the birds and wind and my imagination for company—all of this had suddenly vanished.

The destruction of the woodlands I witnessed in the early 1950s has only intensified since then. Today the vast majority of children in this country are growing up without even a taste of what I was conscious of losing as a child. The natural world has been replaced by an electronic simulacrum, with attendant consequences we are only beginning to understand.

Our documentary explores some of the ramifications of these changes. The freedom to explore I had as a child, my youthful con-nection with nature, all shaped the person I am today and the way I see the world and move through it. It is critical that we examine how the disappearance of play and our diminishing contact with nature are affecting our children and grandchildren. It's for them that I wanted to make this film.

Mark Jonathan Harris is a journalist, novelist, and documentary filmmaker whose work has won three Academy Awards. His first Oscar was for "The Redwoods" (1968), a short documentary he wrote and produced. He also wrote and directed two Oscar-winning feature documentaries: "The Long Journey Home" (1997) and Into "The Arms of Strangers: Stories of the Kindertransport" (2001). In addition, he has published five novels for children, two books of non-fiction, and dozens of essays, articles and short stories in publications ranging from *American Heritage* to the *New York Times*. A professor at the School of Cinema-Television of the University of Southern California, he has taught filmmaking there for 20 years.

# Jeff Kupperman

# MICHIGAN STUDENTS AS DOCUMENTARY FILMMAKERS

**Jeff Kupperman is assistant professor of education at University of Michigan—Flint, and a core member of U-M's Interactive Communications & Simulations group. A major focus of his work involves the development of technology-mediated programs that allow K-12 and university students to push the boundaries of play, communication, social action, and culture.**

Among the fourth grade set, forget McMansions: when looking for real estate, kids go after the smallest space on the block.

This was the trend, at least, that three teams of high school students found when they set out to film elementary age children in their communities. Armed with digital video cameras and microphones, the high school students visited fourth graders at school and at home, asking them about the "secret spaces," both indoors and out, where they go to play, relax, or simply get away. Each team was asked to produce a two or three minute mini-documentary about where and how boys and girls play. Along the way they collected drawings, led class discussions, toured playgrounds, and were invited into back-

7

yards, rooms, and even closets that contain the spaces children call their own.

With coaching from UM-Flint faculty advisors and film producer Donna Ryen, the student teams collected footage over the course of several months, then pulled out themes, created storyboards, and brought everything to Michigan Television studios in Flint for a series of marathon editing sessions. The finished videos can be viewed at michigantelevision.org

We chose three different communities in Michigan: Howell, a historically rural town in the midst of a wave of suburbanization; West Bloomfield, an affluent, established Detroit suburb; and an urban community at the edge of Flint, known for its post-industrial economic woes.

In all three communities children described tiny spaces, often barely large enough to fit their own bodies: the space under a table, the inside of a tire, woods where an opening in the center of thick brush made a "secret park," a hollow tree stump, a closet, and even a cupboard six feet off the floor.

Surprisingly, these tiny territories were most often places where children went to be alone; they rarely functioned as clubhouses or meeting points for friends. They truly were personal spaces. "Can you show us your secret park?" we asked the girl who had described it in splendid detail. "Of course not," she replied. "If I did, it wouldn't be secret!"

One fourth grader, though, was willing to show her secret refuge to two of the teenage videographers: "When I'm sad, I go in here to get away from everybody," she says in the video, as the camera follows her inside a hollow playground tire. "This is where I come in, and I drink my milk inside for lunch, and that gets my creative juices going. For some reason, when I'm out there, my juices don't flow, but when I'm in here they flow, awesomely."

We expected to see differences in where and how children in the three communities play: perhaps kids in Howell, where there is plenty of open space, would play a lot outside; kids in West Bloomfield would be likely to have lots of expensive toys; and outdoor play in Flint might be hampered by a lack of attractive public spaces. What we found, though, was quite a bit different.

In West Bloomfield, where most families have no trouble affording high-tech toys, some kids still managed to find low-tech, improvised spaces to make their own. In the film from this community, one girl smiles from the floor of a closet filled with boxes; another piles blankets under an expensive-looking air-hockey table to make a cozy, dark, tent-like room.

In Howell, Kellie and Meredith, the high school student videographers, were shocked to find that even in the eight years since they were in fourth grade children seem to have moved more and more indoors. More than either of the other teams, Kellie and Meredith were disturbed by what seemed to be a decline in imaginative (and especially outdoor) play—concerns echoed by others in this volume.

"The vast majority of students we filmed preferred to play inside of their house," reflected Meredith. "Even though they live in a traditionally rural community with many places for them to play, they preferred to play inside of their video games, in an alternate reality of sorts. Throughout the project, we were taken aback to find the exact opposite of what we expected, children in Howell no longer prefer to play outside." Meredith's phrase "inside of their video games" is telling: a video game can be a kind private space—sometimes solitary, sometimes social—and perhaps children find a refuge there not unlike the cozy "real" spaces filmed by each of the teams.

In Flint, some kids also liked to play "inside of their video games," but it was here that we also found the most children who claimed wild outdoor spaces as their own—"my grandmother's swamp," one mentioned, or an unnamed clearing at the end of a wooded trail. We speculated that the Flint children—who were actually from an area on the edge of the city—tended to live in more crowded houses with fewer indoor places where they could play undisturbed, and many found that outdoor secret spaces provided a rare bit of solitude and quiet.

These insights were possible, at least in part, because the videographers were close enough to their subjects to understand what it is like to be a kid in their community, yet old enough to reflect on how play and play spaces are changing.

With guidance and technical support from Michigan Television production staff, the students were able to turn these insights into videos that have both polish and youthful energy. "As a producer, I always find it exciting to see young people film and create fresh content," said Donna Ryen, who guided the students' work from pre-production through editing. "The common thread in their work, I find, is a raw truth—always a unique perspective. They

9

express themselves and tend not to hold anything back."

Creating something new, expressing oneself, not holding back—it sounds very much like children at play, and perhaps play itself can connect us together across generations. As Meredith remarked, "Whether it be dancing in the hallways of school, or sneaking a deck of cards into the classroom, we did whatever we could to find time to 'play'. . . . Above all else, we found that play never stops, it just changes as we grow older."

**Student videographers: Dasmyn Langston, Flint/Westwood Heights**
**Justen Lewis, Flint/Westwood Heights**
**Kellie McMillan, Howell**
**Meredith White, Howell**
**Michelle Murphy, West Bloomfield**
**Rebecca Targan, West Bloomfield**
**UM-Flint faculty advisors: Jeff Kupperman**
**Sharman Siebenthal-Adams**
**Gary Weisserman**
**WFUM: Jennifer White, Station Manager**
**Christopher McElroy, Director of Production**
**WFUM production staff: Donna Ryen, Producer**
**Erik Davis, Editor**
**Michael Saunders, Technical Support**
**Steve Kimbrell, Photography**
**Cooperating elementary school teachers: Christine Bradshaw (Hamady Elementary School, Westwood Heights Public Schools)**
**Kristina Parker (Hamady Elementary School, Westwood Heights Public Schools)**
**Lynette Autry (Northwest Elementary School, Howell Public Schools)**
**Sharon Dardarian (Roosevelt Elementary School, West Bloomfield Public Schools)**
**Special thanks to Jay McDowell of Howell High School**

Back Story On Play

In 1893 Frederick Jackson Turner declared that the American frontier was over. Exactly 100 years later the U.S. Census Bureau issued what it said would be the last report on farm families in America because apparently there weren't enough farm families to count anymore. . . .

The second frontier was that kind of romanticized frontier of Teddy Roosevelt in which we thought about nature alot and played in it. And I and other baby boomers caught the tail end of the second frontier . . . . Most of us had an uncle, an aunt, a grandfather, somebody who had a farm and we would go visit them. After my age that pretty much disappeared, and we became a very urban nation. And this has led, I think, now into the third frontier . . . in which we are not sure what life is.

We're now into nanomachines and artificial intelligence. Nature in the third frontier has become a kind of abstraction as opposed to an intimacy in nature. . . . Nature is something you wear on a T-shirt or you buy at a nature store.

*For tens of thousands of years, for all of human history and prehistory, human children went outside and spent much of their lives in nature either working or playing. And within the space of two or three decades in western society, we're seeing the virtual end of that.*

RICHARD LOUV
AUTHOR, *LAST CHILD IN THE WOODS*

Sometimes there were wars. Once there was a great war, boys against girls. Charles and Marian were the generals. The girls had Fort Irene, and they were all girl scouts. The boys made a fort at the other end of Roxaboxen, and they were all bandits.

ALICE McLERRAN, *ROXABOXEN* (1991)

# Joe L. Frost

# AN HISTORICAL IMPERATIVE TO SAVE PLAY

*When I was young in the mountains, I never wanted to go to the ocean, and I never wanted to go to the desert. I never wanted to go anywhere else in the world, for I was in the mountains. And that was always enough.*

CYNTHIA RYLANT
WHEN I WAS YOUNG IN THE MOUNTAINS (1982)

**Joe Frost spent his depression-era childhood in the Ouachita Mountains of Arkansas, playing in the wilderness and working on the farm. He has served as president of the Association for Childhood Education International and as president of the International Play Association USA. He continues to direct a three-decades-old research program on children's play and play environments in Austin, Texas.**

When the first settlers came to America, they brought with them a rich heritage of children's play dating back to antiquity. Throughout recorded history, children played in much the same way until the latter two or three decades of the twentieth century when a radical transformation took place, changing both the context and nature of free, spontaneous play. During this brief period the play of American children came under stress from a collective set of influences that threatened their health, learning, and physical, emotional, and intellectual development. Just how this came about is quite a story, remarkable for its speed and negative impact.

The play of children is extensively documented by archeological remains dating back to pre-recorded eras and in the writing of prominent philosophers and educators throughout antiquity, the medieval and renaissance periods and the pre-modern and modern eras. Country children played in natural surroundings which differed across geographical areas—hills, wilderness, streams, ponds, rivers, fields, plains, barnyards, deserts, and swamps. Not unlike their country counterparts, city children played wherever they happened to be—in streets, vacant lots, shops, factories, back yards, seaports, and in smaller towns and villages, the surrounding countryside. No matter the context or the demands placed on them, children found places and made time for play. They created their own games, made toys from simple, natural materials, played the games passed down for centuries, and cunningly outfoxed adults to transform work into play. The differences between the aristocracy or the well-to-do and the masses living in poverty or under unspeakable conditions have always been profound, but, except in the most brutal conditions of war, abuse, and natural disaster, play found a means for expression.

Remarkably, yet understandably, given play's universality and benefits, even the greatest of the ancient philosophers such as Plato, Aristotle, and Quintilian recognized the importance of play for children and promoted its role in education and development.

Others echoed advocacy of play through the centuries to follow. Luther, Comenius, Locke, Rousseau, Pestalozzi, Herbart, Froebel, and many other great observers and thinkers spoke for play's physical, intellectual, learning, and

moral values and contributed to its centuries-old acceptance and cultivation.

Around the turn of the twentieth century several child-centered movements in America, including the child savings movement, the play and playground movement, and the child study movement led to the development of playgrounds in cities and research on play at universities. By that time the largest cities were crowded, with huge pockets of poverty, and safe outdoor play places were disappearing. Orphans were everywhere in the slums and many children were assigned back-breaking work in factories. Despite such conditions, children managed to play. Country children, having ready access to farms and wilderness, played as country children have always played, having nature itself as a playground, perhaps the finest of settings for free, creative, spontaneous play.

During the final decades of the twentieth century, the age of technology and related cultural factors began to change children's play in profound ways. Children were staying indoors to play with their tech toys, while all the time making regular trips to the refrigerator for junk food. Kept informed about predators waiting just outside the door, and wall-to-wall coverage of child kidnappings and abuse by the media, parents became increasingly fearful, even paranoid, and warned their children to stay inside. Outdoor play in streets and near-by parks was increasingly abandoned. All this was implicated in growing incidence of previously rare health problems, even among very young children—obesity, early signs of heart disease, diabetes, and related emotional and mental disorders.

During the early 1980s national playground safety standards were developed and rapidly implemented, resulting in traditional playground equipment being replaced by new equipment, standardized to meet safety specifications. These specifications gave attorneys the fuel to present elaborate, technical arguments in litigation, frequently resulting in legal judgments against schools, parks, child care centers, and individuals.

By the turn of the twenty-first century, threat of lawsuits had become so pervasive that all parties involved with the development or use of playgrounds were at risk—manufacturers, architects, installers, school administrators, teachers, nurses, and doctors.

Even injuries resulting from contact with common and natural materials on playgrounds such as rocks, tree roots, stumps, and fences, though not classified as manufactured playground equipment, could result in legal scrutiny and potential liability. As the safety standards became ever more extensive, complex, and confusing, playgrounds became more standardized and cookie cutter in appearance and function and were frequently described as "dumbed down," meaning void of challenge and fun.

By 2007, such criticism was resulting in manufacturers searching for ways to circumvent the safety standards or modify them to allow greater heights, greater thrills, and greater challenges and risks, and school districts across the country were deleting or reducing recess and imposing "risk-free" rules on children at play. Traditional games were banned in many places, including tag, chase, dodge ball, tether ball, football, soccer, and in even more extreme cases, all games involving human contact. Perhaps the height of irresponsible, damaging regulation was reached when one school posted signs, NO RUNNING ON THE PLAYGROUND, and some school districts decided not to provide playgrounds at their schools.

Another form of standardization emerged with the passage of the No Child Left Behind Act, or high stakes testing. Created primarily by politicians, this illogical, ill informed program quickly resulted in punitive measures against low performing schools and their teachers, administrators, children, and parents. Researchers found little validity to claims of rapid progress on tests, especially among the poor and minorities, and uncovered wholesale cheating and growing disillusionment and rejection of the program by teachers and parents. The content of tests had become essentially a national curriculum and children's play was not included. The results of the testing mania were widespread and punishing to children.

Recess was abandoned by a growing number of schools to make more time for teaching the tests. Some schools were built without playgrounds, ostensibly to avoid injuries and lawsuits, or closer to reality, because many adults failed to understand the developmental values of children's free play in outdoor playgrounds or were fearful that their schools and children might be designated "low performing." Despite the immense amount of erudition (historical, scientific, sociological, literary) available through the cultural lens of play, the fear of injury, lawsuits, abduction, school failure, and misunderstanding the values of play collectively unraveled centuries of openness to challenging play and play environments, both natural and built, and now threaten the health and welfare of American children and growing numbers in other countries.

There are indications that children's spontaneous outdoor play may be resulting in slowly making its way back up the staircase. The looming threats to nature are influencing groups throughout America to reintroduce children to play in nature, and to cultivation of nature in neighborhoods and school grounds. The National Wildlife Federation certifies schoolyard habitats nationwide. Common Good works to bring common sense back to lawsuits; KaBoom and other organizations construct playgrounds in poverty areas and areas decimated by natural disasters. The Voice of Play prepares papers promoting the values of play for publication in various journals. The Strong National Museum of Play opened in 2007. Legislators are addressing problems of high stakes testing, out-of-control lawsuits, and the need for recess and physical education. Dozens of professional organizations never abandoned their stands for outdoor play and play environments and valid assessment of children's progress, and seek ways to reintroduce reason and scientific study into decisions that affect children. Now we see the "no child left behind culture" gradually being countered by an emerging movement committed to the slogan, "no child left inside."

Is play worth all this effort? The answer is a resounding, "Yes." Perhaps on no other issue in education and child development is the historical and scientific evidence clearer. Play is essential for problem solving, social and cognitive skills, imagination, creativity, therapeutic relief from trauma, passing on culture, and physical development and health. To put it romantically but accurately; spontaneous play is the delicate dance of childhood that strengthens the mind and body, and nourishes the soul. Our task is to save spontaneous, creative, outdoor play and play environments for children.

*A generation or two ago the parents were pretty much hands off. There was not the perception that it was dangerous to be out in the streets if you were in a city. If you were in a rural setting, you generally didn't have an automobile to take you to practice football or volleyball or some such thing, so kids were left largely on their own in the afternoon after school to make up whatever kind of play they wanted to.*

STUART BROWN, FOUNDER / PRESIDENT
THE NATIONAL INSTITUTE FOR PLAY

*The plays of childhood are the germinal leaves of all later life.*

FRIEDRICH FROEBEL, *THE EDUCATION OF MAN* (1826)

# Mary Ruth Moore

## A Monument to Play

*Play is the purest, most spiritual activity of man at this stage, and at the same time typical of human life as a whole—of the inner hidden natural life in man and all things. It gives, therefore, joy, freedom, contentment, inner and outer rest, peace with the world.*

FRIEDRICH FROEBEL (1826)

**Mary Ruth Moore is professor of education at the Dreeben School of Education at the University of the Incarnate Word. Before coming to the university, she spent twenty-five years as an elementary school teacher where she learned the value of play.**

I first saw an old picture postcard of the monument to Friedrich Froebel in Norman Brosterman's *Inventing Kindergarten*. Immediately, I knew that I must see this monument for myself. What was unique about this gravestone in Schweina, Germany? More than eleven feet high, a granite monument was designed by the grandsons of Martin Luther, a testament to what Froebel believed about play. Perched high on the top of the monument are a sphere, a cylinder and a cube, the most readily identified example of Froebel's original teaching blocks. While toys were common playthings in Europe during the 19th century, they were highly stylized, specific and often so realistic that only one purpose could be served. For example, a tower was always just a tower or a horse shaped block could only be a horse. Exploration and discovery were absent from the toys and blocks previous to

Froebel's blocks. Because of the many shapes of these blocks and toys, none were very adequate for building. For his kindergarten classes as well as for use by mothers in the home, Froebel first designed blocks of natural wood for stacking and mathematical connections. His blocks were more open ended as they could serve unlimited purposes. These blocks could be used in mathematics, story time, social studies or any area of the curriculum. For instance, the sphere could represent a person in a story or song and the cube could be a building or a chair. Froebel designed smaller versions of the cube for the active construction of the child. These newly invented blocks would be central to his garden for children or kindergarten, developed from his unwavering belief that play was central to learning.

Now aptly termed "Froebelblick" or Froebel's view, a majestic valley below his home inspired this educational pioneer to envision a new form

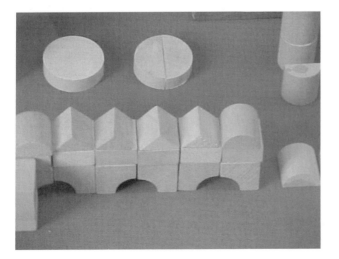

of schooling for young children with play as the key to unlock the imagination. He dreamed of a kindergarten or children's garden filled with the wonders of nature to actively engage the bodies and minds of three through six-year olds. Froebel gave his educational program a series of loose parts or educational materials that he named "Gifts" for learning to occupy little hands. These gifts included yarn balls, the sphere, the cylinder and the cube, a series of unit blocks, a series of geometric shapes, sticks and rings and activities for each. The outdoors and gardens, music and movement, storytelling and rhyme took center stage in kindergarten. The rhymes and rhythm of language and music engaged the young learners. He focused on positive interactions of the mother or teacher singing and playing with the child. For these positive interactions, he designed a new language play genre called fingerspielen, the German word for finger plays. Play with blocks, clay work, drawing, cutting, weaving and folding occupied the children's time. Special days or play fests, the forerunner of play days, a day totally filled with free play for play's sake in the outdoors, celebrated the open-ended, expressive nature of play and the child as a constructive genius.

Today, in contrast to Froebel's vision, toys with one intended use, do little to stimulate the mind, hands, and body. Blocks are noticeably absent from kindergartens and elementary schools. Current educational materials are more often worksheets that require children to "bubble in" the correct answer. Pre-schoolers sit for hours with no time to play or wander outside. In fact, the child's ability to wonder about nature is seemingly forgotten. High-stakes testing appears to be the norm with adults not seeing the obvious link between testing, childhood inactivity, and the epidemic of childhood obesity.

What can we do to improve this dilemma?

What would Friedrich Froebel say to us if he were here today? I think he would urge us to the return to the roots of the kindergarten he envisioned and to reinstate the garden, the outdoors, and most of all, play for all children. He would provide children with blocks that spur imaginative uses. Finally, I believe he would point us to his monument where his famous motto appears, "Come let us live for our children."

# Jeanne Schinto

# THE PALACE OF GREEN PORCELAIN

*I dream I love the simple
and enter the museum of my past*

SUE STANDING, *DECEPTION PASS*

Jeanne Schinto has been an independent writer since 1973. The author of *Huddle Fever: Living in the Immigrant City* (Alfred A. Knopf, 1995), a memoir of the ten years she spent in the old textile-mill city of Lawrence, Massachusetts, she has also published articles on art, history, and the material culture in a variety of publications, including *The Atlantic Monthly, Gastronomica, and DoubleTake Magazine.* From 1998 to 2004, she was a weekly columnist for and regular contributor to the largest alternative newspaper in the country, *San Diego Reader.* Currently she is a correspondent for *Maine Antique Digest,* covering auctions, antiques shows, and the trade.

I bought a diorama. It's an underwater window of a rivershore or a lakefront some where, possibly Great Britain, according to the auctioneer who sold it to me, for $225. That's a good price for a diorama of its size—three feet by two feet by half-a-foot deep—no matter what little rectangle of the world it is trying to depict. The "water" of this 3-D still-life is a murky yellow-brown. It looks the way it would if all the half-dozen fish inside it had heavy nicotine habits. A knowledgeable friend of mine who examined its wooden case guesses that it was built at about the same time as the Titanic.

Age has ruined the long black eel that is lying on the bottom of it. Satisfyingly ugly, it has broken into halves. The pickerel, however, is well-preserved, and so is the pair of perch, placed symmetrically, fin to fin, in the scene's center by the anonymous diorama-maker. That disposition was a mistake in my opinion—the antithesis of underwater reality. But it's redeemed with a bird, at the very top, suspended in six inches of painted "sky." Flying low, over a fringe of faded weeds, the bird lends a verisimilitude to the picture that would be lacking otherwise, by supplying a narrative pull: Poor bird, looking for food. Will he find it? I like the combination of fish and fowl for another reason, too. One represents for me the hidden world, below the surface of things; the other, the world above. I'm always looking for the places where those two worlds meet.

And I've always been drawn in by dioramas. The first ones I ever saw were at the local cabinet of curiosities in my old hometown—the Bruce Museum of Greenwich, Connecticut—founded in 1912, the same year that my own diorama was estimated to have been built. At the Bruce there were dozens of scenes of all sizes, from table models (like mine) to huge, wall-sized, vistas. My best friend, Maureen, and I would go to the Bruce on a rainy Saturday. We were supervised by neither parents nor teachers nor museum guards on these trips, and that was part of the place's appeal. Free to roam the tall, turreted Victorian mansion, a former private home, roam we did, imbibing the strangeness and the familiar made strange. We liked the giant luminous clam shell (the color of the moon), near the foot of a dimly lit stairway. We looked up at it on its pedestal—into its fluted jaw, so to speak—or grew pleasantly dizzy looking down on it from the stairs leading to the Bruce's upper floors. Peering over the banister of the third-story landing, we liked to frighten ourselves by imagining how easy it would be to fall down on top of it. Back downstairs, we made a stop in the room that had been converted to a planetarium: we never tired of having our blouses turned temporarily fluorescent lavender under the magical black light. After that, we visited the little indoor zoo, with its live monkeys that leapt from branch to branch curling their rubbery lips and screaming behind the glass at us. In the 1950s we were already losing touch with nature in Greenwich. Maureen's and my neighborhood was part of the loss—a development of mostly identical houses built almost all at once, during the post-war rush. Its saving grace was that it abutted a golf course where, it was said, foxes lived. We never saw one, ourselves, but we did enjoy the profusion of wildflowers in the roughs between the fairways.

Upon entering the Bruce, we did not feel exactly reverential, the way we felt when we climbed up the stone steps to Mass at St. Mary's. It was closer to the feeling we had when we entered the movie theater downtown, but not quite that, either. This was more serious, like our library mood: the Bruce was certainly the library's next-of-kin, although much more enticing. We loved books, but did so without knowing it—that is, we loved the places books took us. Our minds were fertile; we could imagine our own stories: we didn't always have to read them. So what we loved with a conscious love were other things, other objects, particularly untouchable ones, like the things we saw at the Bruce.

An odd assemblage of paintings and sculpture was also part of the mix, but Maureen and I didn't explore them. Without even stepping inside the gallery, we could see from the doorway The Bust of Eve, a white marble sculpture of Adam's wife. And although, as I recall, it stopped just short of her breasts, the word bust was still too much for us—girls whose own breasts, tender swollen embarrassments, were getting ready to mound. With our heads down, nervously giggling, we hurried past it on our way to the rooms of dioramas. One of our favorites was "May Morning," featuring a doe and her fawns (Walt Disney's Bambi would long remain fresh in our minds). Another, whose name I have forgotten, showed a mother black bear and her cubs. The smaller mammals included in these large panoramas—chipmunks, squirrels, rabbits—were familiar enough to us, from our own backyards as well as our roamings on the golf course. But we weren't accustomed to seeing them motionless—dead. And it was hard to shake the wishful idea that they were still alive (merely stunned was our fiction), having

somehow accidentally wandered into the scene, and were about to start scurrying around in the leaves at any moment. I think, however, that something beyond a mere re-creation of reality made possible the sweet confusion and held us transfixed. At the Bruce the preternatural tones of the painted skies—the effects of aging here, again, as in my fish diorama, perhaps—made the scenes seem otherworldly. The lighting, too, just missed evoking natural light, and this increased the uncanny effect. It was, instead, the light of dreams, somebody else's not ours, and yet we were invited into them, to stay for a while in a kind of mutual dream, which was really better than having one alone. But the dioramas were better, as well, than the Bruce's zoo, because the frenzy of the monkeys, cooped up in their cages, made us feel frenzied, too. Here in front of the dioramas we got tranquilly alert, like two people fishing: we wanted to catch the dioramas' secrets, and these artificial windows on the real world seemed to have an endless supply. On each visit we always found something new. It was the best kind of watching. There were only a limited number of open secrets to be had at the pleasure of the scratching, tumbling, literally crazy monkeys.

These museums adventures of mine had residual effects at home. For example, it was because of the Bruce that I tried to dig for arrowheads in my own backyard. I used a garden hand tool with claws to engage in this dubious

has always differed in nature from individual collecting. But even some large repositories still manage to convey the feeling I'm after. I felt it recently at the British Museum, monstrous though it may be, amid the painted mummy cases. The ancient was somehow brought close to me by these objects and by the simple, unadorned way in which they were displayed. I understand about differing "learning styles," to use the jargon. I know and appreciate the efforts that some museum designers make to reach all kinds of different people and to make museum-goers of them. Still, in London, in that roomful of antiquities, without benefit of exhibition copy or a nattering guide, a barrier was broken. A tunnel backwards was dug. The objects hummed down through the ages. Somehow they signaled their spirits, and I signaled back. It happened again, just a few months ago, at the Peabody Essex Museum in Salem, Massachusetts, in the new whaling exhibit featuring paintings of whaling scenes, harpoons, scrimshaw, whale oil and whale oil containers, ships' log books, maps, much more. Somehow they got it right, without resorting to a little darkened room with a video presentation or anything else too jarringly high-tech. The story was told through the juxtaposition of the artifacts and the actual words of nineteenth-century participants or observers—quotations on the walls—along with the artworks. The proof that it affected me: when I got home, and for days

and days afterwards, I found myself thinking about it—the men, the ships, the whales themselves—and when I could no longer bring the feeling back, I felt compelled to reread a few chapters of my twenty-five-year-old, annotated college copy of Moby-Dick, which now looked to me like a piece of ongoing history, itself.

Doubtless there are still people living in Greenwich who find unusual creatures in their own backyards. But do they bring them to the new Bruce? If I were a "curious" adult living in Greenwich today, I wouldn't consider it. It's not that the people behind the information desk seem capable of rebuffing. (Although they may well be. When I asked, "Where did the giant clam shell go?" one of them issued a curt, "In storage," without offering any further details. Maybe I wasn't the only former town resident to come looking for the old familiar landmarks and, not finding them, looking displeased, maybe even a little dangerous.) It's just that the sleek new Bruce into which they are charged with welcoming visitors hasn't the slightest hint of having been, or wanting to be, adlibbed, much less added to by an amateur. Whether a staff member wanted it or not, I don't think that the careful design could easily absorb a random gift of a snake or a hornets' nest. Not that the Peabody Essex could have absorbed my dog-eared *Moby-Dick*; still, I had the feeling that those who had designed the exhibit would, on some level, have appreciated it.

The original Bruce mansion, it should be noted, is, essentially, gone. As a matter of record, the architects used the old building's structure literally as a base for the new one, making their design decisions in and around it. But, as far as I can see, only its cone-shaped turret remains; the rest has dissolved into an entirely new stucco creation of cream and soft green, with a roof line that advertises Asian influences. Up the front steps, past the plaques listing columns of donors, visitors enter a towering, sky-lit rotunda, where there is no longer any need to wend one's way through a rabbit warren of exhibition rooms and up and down a vertiginous staircase. Instead, they may stroll in and out of a single floor of sleek exhibition space, double the size of the old square footage, on either side of a wide hallway that ends in a wall of glass showing a view of parkland and an atrium graced by an Alexander Calder mobile. It goes without saying, perhaps, that no trace of the little zoo remains, although there is a "touch tank." The old dioramas, also, have been jettisoned, and a solitary new one has been built with the help of a venerable master, one of the best, preparator emeritus of the American Museum of Natural History, Raymond de Lucia (1917-1997).

Not that I hadn't begun to realize, by the time I was a teenager, the true position of the Bruce in the hierarchy of museums, courtesy of school trips to the New York museums and to New Haven's Peabody Museum of Natural History at Yale. Then, in 1969, when I went away to college in Washington, D.C., the Smithsonian became my "local museum," where I often felt that elusive universal connection—for example, while watching the Foucault pendulum knock over the circle of markers as the planet revolved beneath it. And I mostly forgot about the little Bruce. After I got married, we stayed on in D.C., during a period when many museums on the mall were refurbished in time for the Bicentennial and the one that is currently the most visited museum in the country was built: the National Air and Space Museum.

On weekend visits home to see my parents, I sometimes did revisit the old Bruce. I could see that its exhibits were careworn, outdated. I could see, too, that its dingy walls and scuffed floors and poor lighting were ready for refurbishment. At the very least, the place needed to be made handicap-accessible and temperature-controlled. There were also security issues—thefts had occurred, it had been reported in the newspaper.

There was one more important issue, too, reported to me by my ninety-year-old Uncle Dan, who, at the tail end of Paul Howes's tenure, was hired as a custodian at the Bruce. As a boy, he and his siblings—my father, among them—had gone to the Bruce "all the time, all the time," enjoying the live things especially. But while he worked there, people newly enlightened by the animal-rights movement were beginning to complain about the treatment of the monkeys in the little zoo, and in 1980, it closed, as part of a planned general reorganization, according to the front-page article in *The Greenwich Time*.

At about the same time, according to Uncle Dan, more art was starting to be shown at the Bruce, art for which he didn't have much use. For himself, he favored the art of the dioramas, and marveled over the man who had created them: "Paul G. Howes." (Whenever he spoke of him, he would always respectfully include his middle initial.) It was Uncle Dan who told me that, as another part of the reorganization, the dioramas were scheduled to be demolished. I never did get a final look at them.

And that was the end of the Bruce, at least as I knew it, where even art did eventually get introduced to me, in a strange way. It happened on an after-school visit: although the nuns didn't take us, my Brownie troop did, one memorable time. It was 1962. I was in sixth grade. Four years earlier, with compensation money paid to the town after the Connecticut State Thruway cut a swath through Bruce Park and damaged the structure of the old Bruce manse in the process, Howes not only repaired the building, he put on an addition—a two-story cement-colored box, quite ugly by anybody's architectural standards then or now; but, at least, the interior of the upper floor must have pleased those interested in aesthetics: it was reserved for a new art gallery.

We started our tour in the old first-floor gallery, looking at a traveling display of jewelry on religious themes. The artist who had designed the pieces was a Spaniard named Dali. With his slick black ringmaster's moustaches, his impish vampire looks, Dali was already a celebrity by then, but we had never heard of him. I liked saying the phrase "lapis lazuli," and recognized the crucifix and other sacred symbols that the designs incorporated; but the gems themselves didn't hold much interest for me. I went up to the second-floor gallery, where Dali's paintings and drawings were hanging. Some of the other Brownies were already moving from one work to the next—and squealing with laughter.

I can't tell you exactly what I felt upon impact, but thirty-six years later I was able to pick out of a book one of the pieces I distinctly remember seeing that day, Debris of an automobile giving birth to a blind horse biting a telephone. The horse, with its teeth bared, its legs rearing, its tail furled, is biting the receiver of a phone (meant to allay its pain, the proverbial bitten bullet?)—except that it is not exactly a horse. There is an opening in its side, like a carriage door, and one of its legs is a wheel, and part of another leg is a fender. It's obviously a car that is metamorphosing into a horse, although, true, it is a blind one, for its eye sockets are black holes, eyeless, unseeing.

Our minds were used to making sense of Roman Catholic religious symbols and imagery that could be just as surrealistic as Dali's. But here no explanations were forthcoming from either of our troop leaders (doubtless, dismayed), or from any museum guide. But maybe that was better. Maybe it was a good thing that my reaction—pure, unadulterated shock—was unsullied by an analytical preparation or debriefing afterwards.

I wonder now if Dali was just another freak show to Howes. I hope, instead, that he recognized Dali's virtuosity. I hope, too, he realized that a surrealist was the perfect artist to feature at the Bruce, effectively mixing, as surrealists do, the features of the precise real world and of the slippery world of dreams from which all art springs.

In H.G. Wells's *The Time Machine* (1895), the Time Traveler observes that there are no museums in the world of the future, although he does come across a ruin of one. It's called *The Palace of Green Porcelain*, and it reminds him of the Victorian era museums of his time. Assuming it must be some "latter-day South Kensington," he reports that he "found the old familiar glass cases," but since he is at that same moment trying to figure out how to battle the Morlocks, he has trouble becoming much interested in their contents—"old-time geology in decay." He also comes upon a diorama of a tin mine, and hopes that the dynamite is still live—

he could use it against his enemies; disappointedly he discovers that the sticks are only dummies.

Wells's larger point has to do with class inequality and the idea that the upper classes were soft, lazy, effete, as a result of letting the other classes do all the work for them. In his futuristic vision, museums (and libraries, too) were obsolete, not because their designs and philosophies were, but because intellectual life itself no longer existed. If Wells could see what has happened to museums today, he would understand, as we do, that money, not lack of intellectual power, is one big reason why things have changed. A lot of it is needed to run these places today. Of course, too much money can present another sort of problem, I discovered when I visited the new Mashantucket Pequot Museum and Research Center, near Mystic, Connecticut. It opened on August 11, 1998, financed with $193,000,000 in revenues from the tribe's Foxwoods Resort Casino, the largest gambling establishment in the Western Hemisphere. A month later, Bob and I were following a full tour bus along the winding road as we made our approach. When the bus turned into the casino, we went on, to the museum next door.

The space just inside the main entrance is huge, many-storied, with one massive slanted wall of glass that faces a woodlands. The effect is a transparent teepee-like configuration.

We felt instantly dwarfed, while nature felt majestic—the Native American point of view, so distinctly opposed to the way Westerners often think of themselves. So far so good.

We took the elevator down into the basement level for a journey through 11,000 years of history, beginning, James Michener-style, with the ice age. A notable chilliness was in the air. (It was not just our imaginations, the signage informed us). The museum has not emphasized glass cases, and some of the objects inside those that they do have are simulated, because Native cultures do not permit displaying certain sacred artifacts. This is a lesson slowly being learned by museums across the country, formerly insensitive to other cultures' beliefs, guilty of looting sacred burial grounds, now in the processing of returning those artifacts to their rightful places. The word arrowhead, by the way, is not used at the museum: they are Lanceolate Projectile Points, 7,000 to 8,000 years old. They are Neville Points, or Brewerton Points, 4,500 years old. Where did those Anglo names come from? The commentary doesn't say. But it does note that the bow and arrow appeared in what is now the Eastern United States only as recently as about 1,000 years ago. Arrowheads or points, then, are hardly as important a piece of the Native American story as I once thought, and no child will leave here and futilely try to dig up one. But they may better understand than I did that Native Americans did not

simply drop them on the trail, as I once blithely thought they had.

We passed into the first set of dioramas, featuring a simulated mastodon—extinct relative of the elephant—set against a curved painted snowscape. More familiar, though still strange (and extinct), was a model of a giant beaver, about three times the size of the ones we know today. Then there were the wolves—without a piece of glass separating them from us, and the sound of their howling all around us. These special effects sat less well with me, as such things did at Disneyland and Disney World, both of which I visited too late, as an adult.

Then we came upon the first life-size human figures. They are in a sunken, round, open stage, and the scene is a caribou hunt. These eight early Pequot men and women, wearing splendid white animal furs, are stalking their prey with spears to the tune of more sound effects, winds and animals howling. And it's impressive, all right. Still, I found something unsettling about these high-class mannequins, something I could not immediately name.

Visitors are given Acoustiguides for the main event in a huge, open, multi-stage-like space that simulates the outdoors. Overhead, moving across the "sky," unseen Canadian geese are honking, faint at first, then louder, then faint again, just as it happens in reality. There is also the sound of rushing water. But sound effects are the least of it. Life-size models of people are everywhere, fifty-one figures in all, each based on sketches and measurements made of living ancestors of Pequots, stopped mid-task—cooking, hunting, farming, basket weaving—circa 1550. Listening to the Acoustiguide, I learned a lot. I liked the idea that I could push more buttons for an in-depth explanation, or not push them and move on. After the first couple of times, however, I didn't push. These deeper explanations are dramatizations. The "characters" speak. It's frozen theater, and we, the audience, are meant to be part of the scene, without speaking parts of our own. No, it's a giant diorama, and visitors find themselves inside it. So why did I find it off-putting? Isn't that where I've always wanted to be?

How might a child have experienced it? I could not say. How would I experience the old Bruce as an adult? I thought I could answer that question, without a time machine. All I needed was to make a three-hour car ride to a natural-history museum that still looks about as it did at the turn of the century: the Fairbanks Museum in St. Johnsbury, Vermont. Two friends who spent a lot of time in the Northeast Kingdom, as that part of the country is known, had told me about the Franklin and its astounding array of stuffed birds and mammals, all in a fin-de-siècle building right on Main Street in the quaint town. Franklin Fairbanks, president of the Fairbanks Scale Company, was a collector who regularly invited local residents into his St.

Johnsbury home to see his curiosities. Eventually, though, in 1889, his guests outgrew the space, and he decided to establish a public museum.

Architect Lambert Packard designed the building in the Romanesque revival style of Henry Hobson Richardson. Boston's Trinity Church is one of Richardson's best known works. The sandstone-faced Fairbanks, with its deep entrance archway and tower, exudes an ecclesiastical sensibility. Once a visitor is inside, the feeling intensifies under the vaulted, wood-paneled ceiling. I honestly wouldn't have been surprised to hear organ music playing. On one side of the Great Hall are the birds and mammals of Vermont lined up in a yards' long series of glass cases; on the other side, a matching length of cases featuring those of the rest of the world. The collection includes 131 species of hummingbirds alone. The animals are no less impressive, ranging in size from a polar bear rearing menacingly on its hind legs, to an ermine with its delicate prey, a tiny mouse, arranged in its mouth in such a way that the piece of taxidermy really does pass, inexplicably, from craft to art.

And, I'm happy to report, I did easily fall back into my childhood mode as Bob and I and our two friends toured the nearly empty museum that day. But did I say nearly empty? Yes. And for that reason, I came away realizing that the Franklin is a period piece—itself a veritable museum of a museum, emptiness and all. Indeed, one of the reasons why I enjoyed it so much may have been that I had not been in such an empty museum since childhood, when the Bruce was a kind of sacred clubhouse to me. How quiet it was, how conducive to concentration and to that mutual dreaming that I used to experience with Maureen! Similarly, I remember being able to feel much more connectedness in church on an extracurricular "visit" after school, when St. Mary's was empty, than I ever did at obligatory Mass on Sunday, when it was so easy to become distracted by all the coughing, sneezing, and shifting of posteriors on the pews in front of me.

But an empty church is a church in trouble, if not financially, then spiritually; and no public museum, with or without a substantial endowment, can afford to risk that kind of obscurity, either. If tax dollars are being used, it isn't fair; the money would be better spent elsewhere.

Nor was the old indiscriminate shoot-and-stuff-as-you-please approach of Howes and his fellow explorers "fair" to the species they brought home from the bush, many of them now endangered or extinct.

In the end, then, although I do miss the old Bruce and its peculiar charms, I realize now that nobody should try to duplicate it, or the Fairbanks. Their day is done. I'm just sometimes sorry to see what our day has wrought: the banishment of the small, personal vision (yes, even the quirky ones) in favor of the corporate model.

Maybe that's why auctions and antiques shows seem to appeal to me more these days than many museums do. At those venues there's still a congenial hodgepodge, without officious labeling; and sometimes the actual collector is on hand to answer your questions. And of course you can touch the stuff, even buy it, if you like.

The auction where I bought the fish diorama was in Greenwich, where Bob and I had come for a week to help my widower-father empty the family house. Having sorted through nearly fifty years of accumulated possessions and hauled away most of it in my Uncle Dan's big green 1973 Pontiac Catalina—itself a candidate for the dump—we were ready for a little nighttime diversion.

We'd seen dioramas for sale in the past, but not such a big one. They aren't a standard auction or antiques show item for the simple reason that they were never a standard household item. So they're in that category of things that are rare but not necessarily precious. It's my guess that this one did not come out of a museum, at least not a public one, but I can imagine it in somebody's private museum, as, in fact, it is again.

When we got the diorama home to Andover, we put it on top of our upright piano, where it just clears the ceiling. We have a lot of other antiques in our house, but the diorama always elicits comments from visitors. More than one of them has turned to me and asked, "What do you think of it?"—as if Bob were the only one of us crazy enough to crave a diorama.

So far my reply has been a smile, but to myself I say that the piece is more than a curiosity. In my private thoughts I call it "my favorite object." That was the topic I used to give my classes of ninth and tenth graders, when I taught writing for half-a-dozen years. My theory, repeatedly proven, was that these little (500-word) compositions would quickly tell me about my students' inner lives, because the objects they chose were always personally revealing. With subsequent assignments, I would have to give them numerous examples of what I wanted; this assignment they grasped instantly. The only trouble for some of them was deciding among a number of objects or being unsure if a lost or stolen object qualified. Could something that they no longer possessed still be "favorite"?

I always said yes to that question, knowing that what is out of reach can be more meaningful than what is close at hand, provided it has synecdochical properties. It must, in other words, be a part that stands for the whole—an emblem, a symbol of a world—in the case of many of the student choices, a lost world, often unrecoverable.

I consider the fish diorama a representative of a lost world of mine. I admit now what I've known all along: I will not be returning to that place again.

### Sources and Acknowledgments

Paul Griswold Howes's *Hand Book for the Curious* (New York: G.P. Putnam's Sons, 1936); *This World of Living Things* (New York: Duell, Sloan and Pierce, 1959); and *Photographer in the Rain-Forests* (South Norwalk, Conn: Paul G. Howes & Associates, 1969); Susan Richardson of The Historical Society of the Town of Greenwich; Richard Hart, Local History Librarian at the Greenwich Library; Interlibrary Loan at Memorial Hall Library, Andover, Massachusetts; Pyke Johnson; Sarah P. Morris; and Laurence Goldstein, editor of *Michigan Quarterly Review*, in which this essay in a slightly different form first appeared.

*Over the years I formed a collection of bird and mammal specimens. It came mostly from road kill and from birds flying into large windows that were in vogue on the university campus. This led to my love of the art of John James Audubon and admiration of his so-called elephant folio of colored acquaints, an impressive set of which my father drove me to see in Detroit.*

JONATHAN FAIRBANKS

# Jonathan Fairbanks

# A SUMMER DAY ON ISLAND PARK

Jonathan Fairbanks, a grandfather and painter, is vice president of research at *Artfact*, an international online arts and antiques information source. He is also an emeritus curator for the Museum of Fine Arts, Boston.

Collecting passions begin early. Some believe that it is an instinctive or an inherited trait. I believe that while the impulse to collect comes with birth, its development is nurtured through life by observing the collecting achievements of others.

As a child of a sculptor and professor of art at the University of Michigan, I was surrounded at birth with many works of art. The town of Ann Arbor also provided childhood inspiration in the Natural History Museum where massive collections abounded and distinguished professors welcomed me into their laboratories. I learned about the collecting and preservation of bird specimens from Dr. Van Tyne, mammals from Dr. Burt, fossils from Dr. Hussey, and reptiles from Dr. Blanchard. The Museum's outdoor public display of a Michigan woodland pond was special. It took little persuasion to enlist me as a "child collector" to keep it stocked with live specimens of turtles, frogs, snakes and other creatures discovered and gathered in nearby woods, rivers, lakes and ponds.

One summer day in the early 1940s while hiking with a friend to Island Park on the Huron River, we found a shady spot to eat lunch. Having finished, we looked around for a waste bin in which to toss our paper bags. Instead, to our great delight, we found a warm marshy meadow nearby populated with thousands of newly born garter snakes. Garter snakes bear their young live; they do not lay eggs. The snakes were small and easy to catch. Instead of trashing our bags, we used them for collecting many young snakes. Walking home with heavy bags became a chore. So we caught a bus and paid our nickel fare. Once on the bus, one bag after another broke open to release the wiggling captives. This caused panic among most passengers who rang the bell to get off. Some professors at the back of the bus seemed not to mind. They remained seated, smiling and calmly smoking their pipes. But the bus driver did not appreciate our cargo. He unceremoniously dumped us off while brushing out whatever loose snakes he could find on the bus. I do not recall exactly what he said, but the tone of his voice was not pleasant. For young collectors of living things, be advised that your containers must be secure. Paper bags with moist bottoms do not hold. Also, a bike is better transport for living specimens than a bus.

Parts of this essay originally appeared as a newsletter from *Artfact* magazine.

Public Spaces and Inclusive Play

*What you have are these sort of pod communities*

*placed remotely as we're sprawling further and further*

*away from city centers. Kids are interacting with each*

*other differently, not interacting very much at all in a*

*kind of community way where they just go out and play*

*and ride their bikes and get together in a block. Kids are*

*spending a lot more time in isolation at home. They're*

*playing their Playstations. . . . individualized activity*

*for them when they really need to be socializing more.*

ROBIN MEANS COLEMAN
ASSOCIATE PROFESSOR OF COMMUNICATIONS STUDIES
UNIVERSITY OF MICHIGAN

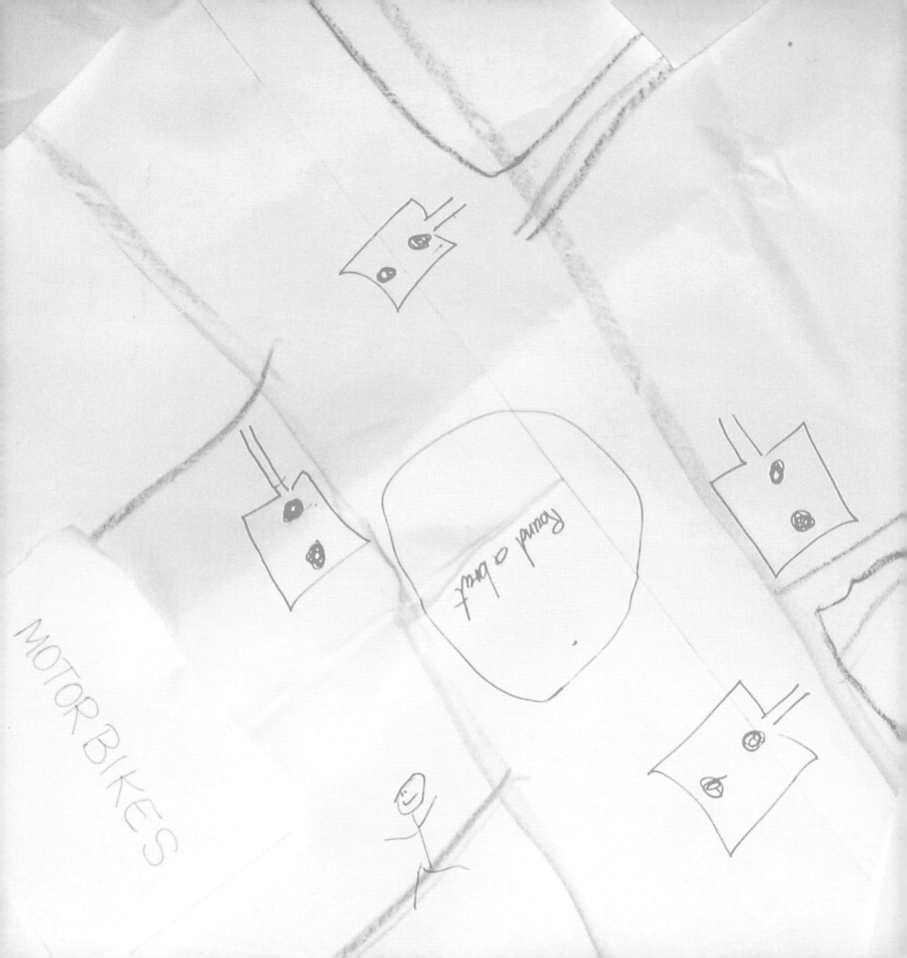

MOTORBIKES

Round a bout

## Claire Gallagher

# IF CHILDREN RULED THE WORLD

## Diversity and Urban Design

Claire Gallagher is associate professor of education at Georgian Court University in Lakewood, New Jersey. She is a trained architect whose research focuses on children and the built environment. Her work includes projects with Frank Lloyd Wright's Fallingwater, the Carnegie Museum of Art, the Heinz Architectural Center, the Cleveland Museum of Art, the Rhode Island School of Design, the Charter High School of Architecture and Design of Philadelphia, and many K-12 schools. Her publications include "'Our Town': Children as Advocates for Change in the City," "Urban Lanscapes and the Visual Culture of School," "What Does an Architect Do?" and "The View of the Child: Explorations of the Visual Culture of the Made Environment" (with Catherine Burke, Ian Grosvenor, and Judy Torrington).

In the summer of 2005, a group of 20 seven- to eleven-year-olds in Sheffield, UK were asked by researchers from The View of the Child Research Cluster[1] to design a city. These children attended an inner-city school and represented the diversity of the residents of their neighborhood. Their teacher had been asked to choose children for inclusion in the project on the basis of their apparent disaffection and lack of inclusion in school activities. She was directed to select students who were never chosen for anything, and who were either limited in their ability to communicate with their classmates through issues of language, or who were ostracized as a result of cultural issues or for something as simple as being overweight or being perceived by their peers as bookwormish or "dorky." As a result, the participants in the project represented an unusually wide variety of abilities and disabilities, ethnicities, socioeconomic groups, cultures, experiences, ages, developmental levels, and interests. Some were refugees, some having arrived in their new homes days or weeks before. Some spoke little English, some spoke none. Some had seen great horrors in their young lives as a result of living in places like Somalia, Iraq, or Iran. Some of the children were from ethnic groups that had been the oppressors of other children in the class. The diversity of this collection of children could not have been more extreme, yet the city they designed could not have been more holistic.

A relaxed non-hierarchical atmosphere was established at the outset of the first day. All participants, children and adults, wore nametags indicating their first names, by which all were addressed. This helped to mitigate the perception of an inherent hierarchy between adults and children. Through such deliberate mechanisms a casual atmosphere of play was established and reinforced throughout the three days of the exercise. The children worked until they finished as much of the city as possible within the timeframe available, which was, according to their comments, not nearly enough. Architecture students from the University of Sheffield and members of the interdisciplinary team from the research "cluster" documented the process and product of the children's experience throughout the exercise.

The first day began with a discussion among the children as to what might be in a city, either real or imagined. The adults helped to encourage the discussion and all suggestions were recorded and placed on pieces of paper that were affixed to an "idea wall." When the list was completed, the children eagerly ran to the wall, choosing buildings, and then placing the papers on a twenty by forty foot basemap where they negotiated final locations and then taped the labels to the appropriate "sites." This process continued until all the brainstormed city elements were sited and the students were comfortable with the final locations. They then chose buildings to design in three dimensions, using recycled materials that they had sorted and stored at the side of the room, off of the map. The adults were there merely to assist when necessary, not to direct any of the children's activities. For some of them this became a learned skill, not an easy one at that. The researchers responsible for the project instructed the adults to avoid falling into their usual patterns of taking over a task, but it was necessary to occasionally remind them as they assisted the students with the project. The children also had some habits to break. It was necessary for them to adopt an unfamiliar dynamic with the adults. Even though they had not met most of the other people they encountered the first day, they had spent so many days in school that they had internalized the behavioral expectations of that place, and had the tendency to fall into a familiar role as well.

At first the children were surprised that they did not need to ask for permission to "play" on the map. Several children were heard to say, "Miss, can we cut this? Miss, can we start?" Gradually there were less and less "Miss" and "Mister" references and, although respectful, the students began to assume the roles of competent designers, no longer needing the approval of the "teachers" in the room. This was an unusual circumstance for them in that they had had little to no prior experience with autonomy and freedom in school and they were reluctant to take a risk for fear of the typical consequences. Interestingly, it took the children less time to shed their

perceptions than it did the adults. Indications of this took the form of comments such as, "It was different; we had to tell the adults what to do." The paradigm had apparently begun to shift.

The first building to take shape was the power plant, designed by a quiet boy, considered to be a loner who set to work on the edge of the city, near the sea, and described his design as he worked. He had a very clear idea of what the function of this complex was and its importance in sustaining the life of the city. Gradually, other children began to design and build around him and although he engaged the adults in a discussion about his idea of connecting electrical wires to the other buildings he would not ask the other students if they wished to do so. Instead, he tried to convince the adults to do it for him. When they refused and he was left with no other choice, the boy began to approach other children and timidly asked, "Would you like to have 'lights' in your building?" and was also quick to add that the power would be free. He was visibly surprised, and pleased, that they were interested in investigating the possibility. This led to a discussion as to how this might be accomplished and much to the boy's delight, the others were eager to connect their designs with his. As time went on he began to try new approaches such as when he was heard to say, "Get power now, get a teddy bear." Later in the day, when children were placing the remaining projects on their respective locations on the map, the boy proudly sat on the floor next to his building watching the activity around him. Things had changed. This disenfranchised child had found that the process of design could serve as an effective interface with the other children, with whom he had difficulty speaking and relating otherwise. As of that moment, his confidence had begun to grow.

Another boy found the same outlet for interaction in designing the public transportation system. He had begun be overcompensating for his isolation from the others by refusing to complete the brainstorming exercise and move on to the placement of buildings at the beginning of the project. He continued to talk, mainly to himself, and when asked by another member of the group about what building he would like to place on the map he moved under a table and tried to brainstorm more on his own. When the attention was turned to one of his concepts, he moved to sit around the map with his classmates to speak about his concerns and to describe what he intended to do. The boy had recently immigrated from Iraq, and his sense of isolation and fear were acute. This was evident during preliminary brainstorming when he had become fixated on incorporating security measures such as CCTV, checkpoints, various modes of surveillance (especially near the sea), gates, and walls throughout. His visceral reaction to issues such as the city's proximity to the sea and his perception of the lack of monitoring of airports, trams, and streets were palpable and led to his insistence on a focus addressing his concerns in the overall city design. Throughout the exercise, he was vigilant about monitoring the other children's work and contributed suggestions when he felt they were necessary to keep everyone safe.

This boy's project began as a monorail and, through an exchange of ideas with other children, became a rollercoaster, and subsequently a waterslide that wove through the city connecting other areas and buildings. This was such a large and ambitious project that he needed to solicit help from others, and his initial attempt was with the adults. In time, he became very critical of the their work and decided that children would be a better choice for collaboration because, "There is a problem with the rollercoaster that the adults have built. There is no up and down; it is not a rollercoaster." From that point on, the design was managed by the boy and constructed by his classmates. There was an inher-

ent hierarchy embedded in this process, one that this boy may have needed as a result of living in such a helpless state in his country of origin. He had, nonetheless, discovered a very effective rationale for engagement with his peers.

The necessity for compromise in this process, as well as certain personalized issues, generated important exchanges between children. For example, one group of Muslim girls had decided to design a mosque but were specific about it being only for "ladies," while a group of their male counterparts intended to do the same for men. It was clear that the issues of the size and placement of the buildings were critical to the perception of equality in the minds of the children, especially for the girls. The subsequent conversation, although subdued, continued for some time. As of the beginning of the building design phase, nothing had been resolved.

The rollercoaster proved pivotal in the placement of other buildings, some far away from the city center. Several children noticed that noise would be a problem, especially for specific functions. The two groups who were still constructing their mosques were unaware of this and were in the "painting room" finishing their work. The boy who had designed the waterslide was walking around the room asking, "Who is making the mosque?" When he discovered that that team was in the adjacent room, he interrupted them and said, "People will be screaming. You need to move it." After considerable discussion, it was decided that rather than reroute the public transportation they should move the mosques. The conversation then became one of "Which is big and which is small?" The girls had designed a larger building that they had painted bright purple, while the boys' mosque was more modest in size and paint choice. The group settled on the fact that one of the girls was more

responsible for the execution of the design than the other, and conceded the choices to her. One boy said, "It is her model; she must decide." The "ladies" mosque was placed in a quiet place closer to where people lived while the boys' building was nearer to the city center, farther away from the residential area.

Some children found safety in their new city, and in the process of making it. When asked they noted that in order to design their city they must, "cooperate, think, and agree." At the end of the two days, the teacher remarked that children who had a history of classroom trouble, poor self-esteem, and a lack of confidence did not exhibit such tendencies during the project. One boy had a tendency to cry often in school and rarely stayed on task for long. He worked alone but did not cry at all during the three days of the project. He chose an airplane and a hotel for his projects, smiled while he worked, spoke shyly but calmly to adults and to other

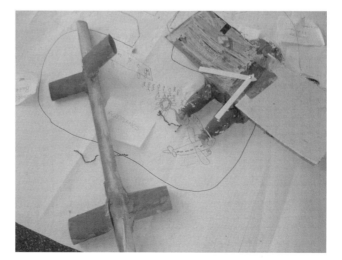

children, and when he had finished making his plane he "flew" it all around the city. He then drew little passengers on the map on the site of the airport and placed his plane carefully next to them.

Several children designed elements of transportation: two airports, one local and one international; the road system, railways, a system of "mermaid taxis" in the sea, and a fleet of flying limousines. Most hubs were located on the pe-

riphery of the map, connected by an easily controlled connection with a major roadway. This was a result of the intervention of the Iraqi boy whose input affected many such decisions.

Infrastructure was also an area of interest, particularly for the boys. A source of electricity was being designed by one individual, but it was established that water would be free and that public transportation would be accessible to all who lived in the city. The group remarked that they would have preferred to have drawn all the streets

themselves, but given that they had been given a basic map derived from the familiar elements in their actual neighborhood, they set about to draw in the rest of the city fabric. One child literally walked the streets assessing where stoplights should be placed so that, as he said, there would be "no crashes." In order to address the concern for convenience for all of the residents, another boy traveled the city adding phoneboxes where people would perhaps find themselves without a phone.

There were also arresting, poignant occurrences during the three days. In the initial brainstorming the children identified the need for a school and an "unschool." When asked what the latter might be they explained that it was a place where "you go outside and know everything, and come back in." The reference here was, of course, to being away from school, where they would learn most things anyway. In the final city design, the piece of paper with the word "school" on it remained in a blank white area, undesigned. The "unschool" areas had been imagined and built throughout while they had repeatedly stepped on the marker for the institution of "school" in the process.

The children were concerned about conflict and integrated elements in their city such as a "make up place where you go after a falling out with a friend." They were also very aware of the needs of others and expressed a concern about "people with sticks," "people who cleaned the city," and a desire to design a place where "money grew on trees" for people who were poor.

The children were interested in the flags of the other children's home countries. Several students went to their classmates and asked them to draw the motifs for them, which they then used in their building designs. One group of boys made a hotel in the shape of a fish and decorated the outside with the flags of the countries of the other children. Others were aware that not all of the group could speak English or communicate easily with their peers. A team of seven year-

old Chinese girls, collectively speaking minimal English, built a language school where one could learn all languages. This school was in the shape of a typical Chinese building but with a twist; you wore the building on your head in order to learn. The girls demonstrated this, dancing around with joy while they did.

As the city was nearing completion the children decided that their city needed a flag and a welcome sign. Both adults and children joined in the discussion. When the conversation became one about what form these might take, a child corrected an adult and said, "You forgot one word: Our." The collective, holistic sense of the city was alive, and the intention of the children was to make it evident to all. A child solicited ideas for a name for the city and a vote was taken. A welcome sign was made and a new flag was designed using elements of all of the children's original maps. These were drawn on a sheet of cardboard and held by the students when the group photo was taken at the end of the exercise.

In their work the children demonstrated a strong sense of community and a clear vision of what their ideal city might be. They had designed their urban environment as a team, not as a collection of individuals. Their new "neighborhood" was defined by its physical boundaries, some defensible, but the people were the fabric of the "place." They were aware of each other, respectful of each other, and indicated no hostility or prejudice toward each other. Their play had generated their vision of a comfortable and safe environment in which they could live, learn, play, and get along. There was no hidden agenda. It was simply a representation of peace.

So what does this all mean? Issues of multiculturalism and diversity do not appear to affect children in the same way they do adults. Children design for each other, not for themselves.

They know the difference between neighborhood and community. They do not come to the table with a political agenda. They are sensitive to the needs of others. They prefer to work together, not individually. They are aware of deficiencies in their immediate environment, both physical and social, and are able to communicate these things to others. They can organize each other and complete a complicated task in which they create a representation of an ideal place for everyone to live.

What's missing? We are. Children have an uncanny ability to see what adults have forgotten how to see. Adults have a tendency to sleepwalk through their built environment while children live in it, are aware of it, and imagine changing it. What adults may consider essential, children may consider irrelevant, unnecessary, or superfluous. Adults often see the glass half-empty while children perceive it as half-full. Adults muster on anyway, inspired by their vague, sometimes romanticized, memories of childhood. They know the answers and act with the best of intentions to protect the young and to provide them with opportunities to grow and develop into responsible citizens. But do they remember what it actually is to be a child? Can they see the world through their eyes? Is that even possible? Are they always presenting the best models of tolerance, awareness, and holistic sensibility? Why not ask children what they would do to make their world a better place? Imagine what might happen if children could dream and adults listened.

*Notes*

[1] The View of the Child research "cluster" was named so as to reflect the diversity of the members of the group who met in a series of "exchanges" designed to create an interdisciplinary interface and to generate a dialogue across disciplines. The goal of the cluster was to explore issues of children's rights vis-à-vis concepts such as advocacy, efficacy, and participatory school design.

## Roger A. Hart

# WILDLANDS FOR CHILDREN

## Consideration of the Value of Natural Environments in Landscape Planning

**Roger Hart is a professor in the Ph.D. psychology and geography programs of the Graduate Center of the City University of New York and director of the Children's Environments Research Group (www. cerg1.org). His research has focused on understanding the everyday lives of children and youth. He has been particularly concerned with the practical applications of theory and research to the planning and design of children's environments and to environmental education. In 1978 he published *Children's Experience of Place*, a natural history of children's lives in a New England town, followed by the BBC/Open University film "Place and Play." Having worked again with this town, and with the original children and their children, he will soon publish a comprehensive study of how childhood has changed. With UNICEF he has published *Children's Participation* and co-authored *Cities for Children*. With Save the Children he has published *Children's Environmental Rights* and the film "Mirrors of Ourselves."**

Landscapes are, in part, expressions of culture, and they support the continuance of particular cultures or subcultures. When one looks closely at variations in landscapes and their different impacts upon children, it becomes clear that they serve as important tools in the socialization of children, though neither parents nor planners are usually conscious of this fact. This essay describes some of the ways that landscapes influence children's development and discusses options open to landscape planners for improving the quality of children's play opportunities.

Usually landscape planners think of gross motor activity when they think of planning and design for children: running, jumping, swinging, and climbing. Exercise is seen as important to the physical health of children. If one simply reflects upon one's own childhood, however, it becomes clear that this is a limited view. It is equally important to consider opportunities for diversity of sensory experience and aesthetic development; competence and autonomy through freedom to explore and manipulate the environment; cooperation with others; and the non-formal experience of other living things. Many of these social and psychological domains can only be provided by landscapes that children can reach by themselves in their own free time. Richer parents often drive children to distant play places and to natural settings, and in some cases this routine probably substitutes for the lack of free play opportunities at home, but it is a qualitatively different experience to be dependent upon chauffeured recreation: a defining characteristic of play —that it is spontaneous and self-generated—implies a freedom for children in space and in time.

The desire of parents to maintain attachment with their young children leads them to require that they play within calling distance of their home (Hart, 1979). Ideally, this range of freedom is gradually extended as the parent and the child gain in competence and confidence (Hart, 1978). Two factors that determine whether or not a child can find suitable places to play close to the home can both be seriously affected by planning policy: spatial accessibility and the types of physical landscapes available. I will focus primarily upon the second of these two policy areas after first briefly summarizing the issue of accessibility.

## Children's Access to the Landscape

Children's freedom to explore the environment is in part a reflection of the different child-rearing ideologies and practices of parents, and these vary greatly in relation to culture, social class and a child's gender. But accessibility is also influenced by other factors beyond the family, notably traffic, crime, and social dangers. The type of residential environment (that is, housing layout and landscape design) can also have a marked impact on freedom of movement. For example, in high rise dwellings, which fortunately are no longer being built for families in Northern European countries, it is impossible for children and parents to negotiate the gradual expansion of children's spatial range which is a characteristic of healthy development and increasing autonomy of action in childhood (Hart, 1979).

Many suburban housing schemes enable children to have a relatively large spatial range. First, there are the landscape qualities that combine to provide excellent visual access: mild topography, absence of vegetation other than lawns, and low density of buildings. Second, there is the relative quiet of the neighborhood coupled with the presence of other parents that commonly enables shouting to be an effective means of communication. Third, there are usually a high proportion of families with children. Not only does any single child not need to travel far to find playmates, but parents also rely upon children of different ages to watch out for one another and to serve as messengers from impatient parents to call in children absorbed in play some distance from home. In areas with a critical mass of families, older children often share the responsibility, implicitly and occasionally explicitly, of watching over children to whom they are not related. This role demands little extra effort because children commonly form themselves into small gangs of relatively stable groups. An additional factor not related to landscape planning but to housing policy is that the suburbs are usually culturally and socio-economically homogeneous, removing the social and cultural prejudice which has also been found to be important in parents' restrictions of children's movements (Hart 1978; Moore 1982). These are some of the influences on children's access to the landscape. More important in this essay for landscape planners is the other half of the question: how do children use the landscape and what do they value in it? That is, what types of places should be accessible to children? In this respect, suburbs often do not score highly at all.

## Children's Use of the Landscape

Remarkably little is known about children's use and experience of the landscape; we know more about the ecology of baboons! What little research has been done has been usually limited to surveys of where children play rather than asking children or by closely observing them (for a comprehensive example of such surveys, see Littlewood and Sale, 1973). The research has been able to offer us some useful information about the location of play, notably that children spend very little time in spaces designed for them such as playgrounds. More detailed studies involving children are still quite rare. The first study known, in German (Muchow 1933), is now primarily of methodological and historical impor-

tance. I will be drawing from the only other studies I know: Southworth (1976), Lynch (1979), Moore (1982), and Hart (1974, 1976, 1979). The high degree of agreement among the four of us I summarize from these observations.

Children use the total landscape accessible to them, and so it is necessary to think of them in the design of the entire outdoor physical landscape of residential areas. A remarkably small percentage of children's free time is spent in playgrounds. Playgrounds are fine for some gross motor activities and excellent for very young children with their parents but satisfy none of the important domains of child development described above.

The spaces that young children value for much of their play are typically smaller in scale than many environmental planners and designers seem to recognize. In order to plan environments that anticipate the diversity of children's interests, as well as their limited spatial range of free movement, it is necessary to think of landscapes with much "finer grains" than the blanket-like suburbs that we have been providing to date.

The most valued spaces for children are typically those that are forgotten by planners and others who provide for children's play. Ironically, the best landscape for children is often one that has been left to the power of nature. Some of the most valued features are: water, sand or dirt, trees, bushes, and tall grass, variable topography, animal life, "found" resources such as berries or fruits and "loose parts" to manipulate and build with. A central rationale given for moving to the suburbs is that they are excellent environments for children, but usually these very qualities are systematically removed from new suburban residential areas.

Children place great value in being able to find and make places for themselves (Hart 1978). This freedom is a rather radical challenge to landscape planners. It has been recognized to a very limited degree through "adventure playgrounds," but these meet the needs of a very small proportion of children. For the very large number of children living in suburban or urban settings, adventure playgrounds with play leaders (now 'playworkers') cannot be provided in sufficient number. A less expensive and better alternative would be to leave "wildlands" or common land that are not planned or manicured for children to make into their own play settings.

## Nature and Children's Development

Many authors and poets have written of the special relationship children have with nature. Froebel and others tried to build this notion into an educational philosophy. What is this special bond? Some say it is based on an open-mindedness and plasticity to the world that is the source of creativity found in children and adults as artists (Cobb 1959). Another suggestion is that there is an existential dimension: children are more interested in the physical world as pre-teens because it is related to their phase of development: that is, they are seeking an understanding of the diversity of the total world, including plants and animals and their place within this scheme (Searles 1977). According to this position, teenagers are more concerned with developing a sense of their own individuality in relation to their peers; they are particularly concerned with other people rather than with the non-human environment. Contemporary psychologists and social scientists usually shy away from discussing the value of nature experiences to child development, probably because of the strong romantic heritage this issue has. However, when we observe the kinds of deep engagement with nature that children have when they are allowed to explore natural settings in non-formal ways, our intuition alone should tell us that this connection is important. My own observations are that small ponds are particularly valuable places for the kinds of quiet "play" of children alone, described by Cobb.

Beyond benefits to individual children we must also adopt, I think, the larger human developmental perspective that in order to understand and value our complex, interdependent life on this planet, it is necessary for mankind, and hence for children, to gain a perspective through experience with other living things. Books, films, museums, and even direct experience with arboretums and zoos are not likely to suffice. Children learn best when they are able to discover things themselves, in their own space and their own time. Present planning policies in North America provide for children many almost identical playgrounds with play equipment, a few large parks, and the occasional trip to a zoo or even a state park or forest. There may well be alternatives. What, for example, would be the value of systematically preserving small areas of residual forest land as common land adjacent to new housing areas, as the fringes of megalopolis expand and its interstices are taken up? What would be the value of mini parks in cities, sufficiently small to be provided every few blocks and colonized by fast growing plants and trees? What if we attempted to preserve ravines through our cities with a minimum of landscaping?

## Rural, Suburban and Urban Landscapes Compared

Rural areas, particularly small towns and villages, have most of the physical landscape qualities valued by children, and commonly offer great freedom to explore and utilize these spaces. They even offer gardens for many children —too difficult to provide in urban areas in large numbers. But rural children complain of the lack of some qualities of city environments: streets or other flat, hard-topped surfaces for cycling and ball games, sports fields and a shortage of other children to play with! But small rural towns are not the kinds of environments landscape planners are being asked to work in. The bigger problems lie in the suburbs and the cities.

Parents in suburban housing areas commonly allow their children to have a larger spatial range because these areas are commonly culturally, socially, and economically homogeneous, relatively free from crime, and have a smaller amount of slower moving traffic. However, the landscape is dominated by adults: the water is drained or covered, sand and dirt are covered with carpets of manicured grass, mature trees are removed and replaced with delicate shade trees, topography is flattened, all loose parts are removed, and much animal life is restricted by creating a monoculture of lawns. Once built, most house owners continue this pattern, although in mature suburbs children sometimes manage to find a few overgrown bushes and trees for use in spite of adult restrictions. The snow also brings relief to many suburbs of North America. The recreational spaces provided by planners in these suburbs are usually limited to sports fields and playgrounds. Both in the USA and the UK, the most valued place to suburban children is "wasteland" —an area that is sometimes accidentally left to nature. Landscape planners should leave small spaces "unplanned" close to housing areas. These spaces would be neither parks nor nature conservation areas but something in between: "common lands" or "wildlands." This concept would be hard for many landscape and recreational planners and managers to accept. Much of the planning and management of these spaces can be largely left to the work of nature: the danger of turning them into "gardens" is real. Ideally, there would be networks of these spaces: leaving valleys and ravines in new housing areas would be one way of achieving this effect.

Suggestions for "natural" spaces in urban areas are more difficult of course because of the high density of the population. "Adventure playgrounds" and "urban farms" satisfy a lot of the requirements, but both require management by adults and cannot be provided in sufficient number for easy access by all (Benjamin, 1974; Bengtsson, 1972; *Childhood City Newsletter* 1978, 1981). Large urban parks are not sufficiently accessible, and they suffer from growing fears of crime. One possibility is the creation of small common lands or wildlands next to community managed space, such as an elementary public school or a garden. Washington Environmental Yard in Berkeley, California, is a wonderful example of what can be done when a community takes control of some of its own landscape planning (Moore 1974).

**A Challenge for Landscape Planning Practice**

This essay has made some bold suggestions for landscape planning from the perspective of a children's advocate, with no discussion of the many other factors that planners have to consider that might limit the possibilities. But these ideas are in line with the thinking of those many planners who believe that we should proceed more ecologically in our planning practice. It has been my goal to argue that as we move to more ecological planning, we must consider children for they have no voice of their own. One of the issues that will certainly need to be faced is the question of how children affect natural systems when they play freely in them. Children frequently want to manipulate their settings, but their interaction with nature is usually gentle—not vandalism, but learning through exploration and experimentation. We need to know more about the ability of plant and animal life to withstand the impact

of use by children if we are to create areas with a high density of use. Specific suggestions concerning the scale and distribution of "wildlands" could easily be made after surveying the existing "accidental" spaces in suburban areas and measuring their "carrying capacity" for children. It is remarkable that no such human ecological research on children's impact on vegetation has, to my knowledge, been conducted. Some of the most ugly "play environments" are now being created because of the financial needs of minimal maintenance: concrete and steel sculptural playgrounds that look modern but have none of the qualities described here. In the "wildlands" proposed here, maintenance would be replaced by "management," an important new job for ecologically-minded landscape planners.

**Postscript:** After giving this lecture I was particularly excited to discover that a "wildland" had been recently created by a planner for a suburban community in Utrecht in the most densely settled country of Europe—the Netherlands. This was truly a wildland, with freedom for children to use as they please. It was managed by the community and monitored for children's safety through regular rounds of visits by parents.

**Originally published in *Landschaft Und Stadt* 14, (1), 34-39, 1982 © Eugen Ulmer GmbH & Co., Stuttgart, this paper was prepared as a Commemorative Lecture in Landscape Planning for the 150th anniversary of the Foundation of the University of Hanover in 1981. Nevertheless, the issue of chil-**

dren's free access to natural environments has become even more of a problem than it was almost three decades ago. On the basis of research in the 1970's with children in New England and New York City, I have found parents' fears of traffic were still dominant amongst the set of forces that led them to restrict their children's freedom in space (Hart, 1978; 1979; 1987). Since that time there has been a sharp increase in parents' fears for children's social safety, in particular the predation of strangers. My comments in this essay hark back to a time when children still commonly played freely outdoors in the public spaces around their homes without adult surveillance. In the suburbs, many mothers were not at work and safety was achieved in parents' minds, sometimes through a kind of collective care with other parents and sometimes from the knowledge that children watched out for one another. Now, as I visit a town that I studied very closely in the 1970s, I am learning that for those parents who try to offer their children "free play" opportunities, it has become an even more complex affair (Hart, 2005).

## Literature

Benjamin, J, 1974: *Grounds for Play*. London: National Council for Social Service/Bedford Square Press.

Bengtsson, A. 1972: *Adventure Playgrounds*, New York: Praeger.

*Childhood City Newsletter*, 1978, 1981: "Special issues on adventure playgrounds and city farms." Center for Human Environments. City University of New York, 365 5th Ave, New York, NY 10016, USA.

Cobb, E., 1959: "The ecology of imagination in childhood." *Daedalus: Journal of the American Academy of Arts and Sciences* 88, 537-548.

Cooper, C., 1974: "Children in residential areas; guidelines for designers." *Landscape Architecture Quarterly*, (5), 372-377 (special issue, "Children know best").

Froebel, F., 1887: *The Education of Man* (trans. by W. M. Hailman). Published by Appleton, New York. (First written in German, 1826).

Hart, R. A., 1974: "The genesis of landscaping." *Landscape Architecture Quarterly* 65, (5), 356-363 (special issue: "Children Know Best").

Hart, R. A. 1976: "Place and play: transforming environments." Program notes for BBC's Open University television program. Milton Keynes, England: The Open University.

Hart, R. A. 1979: *Children's Experience of Place*. Irvington Publishers, New York. Distributed in Europe by Wiley, Chichester.

Hart, R. A. "Exploring the Environment." In Jacqueline Tyrwhitt (Ed.) *The Child in the World of Tomorrow* (Proceedings of the Athens International Symposium). New York: Pergamon Press, 1979. Also published in the special issue of *Ekistics* on children, Summer, 1979.

Hart, R. A. 1987: "The Changing City of Childhood." Publication of the Annual Catherine Maloney Memorial Lecture, City College of New York.

Hart, R. A. 2005: "The Changing Geography of Childhood." Washington DC: National Science Foundation research proposal.

Lukashok, A. K. and Lynch, K., 1956: "Some childhood memories of the city." *Journal of the American Institute of Planners* 22, 152-162.

Lynch, K., 1979: *Growing Up in Cities*. MIT Press, Cambridge, Mass.

Moore, R., 1974: "Anarchy zone." *Landscape Architecture Quarterly* 65, (5), (special issue, "Children Know Best").

Moore, R. 1982: *Children's Domain: Play and Place in Child Development*. Croom-Helm, London.

Shepard, P., 1977: "Place and human development." In *Children, Nature and the Urban Environment*. Proceedings of a symposium-fair, WSDA Forest Service, Upper Darby, Pennsylvania. USDA Forest Service General Technical Report NE-30.

Southworth, M., 1976: "An urban service for children based on Cambridgeport boys' conception and use of the city." Unpublished Ph.D. dissertation. Massachusetts Institute of Technology.

Wilkinson, P., 1979: *Play in Human Settlements*. Croom-Helm, London.

*Children that I see now who haven't got experience playing with children with disabilities actually are quite worried about being cool: if they let go, are they going to be judged to be not quite right, not quite proper?*

*. . . . I took a big box of dressing up clothes into a park, and we were working with half a dozen children with complex needs. I opened the box up and all the children dived in and pulled out stuff, and there were flippers, and top hats, and sparkley dresses, and wings and—you couldn't imagine. It was a real mishmash of stuff. And they all dressed up in these mad outfits, and the children with disabilities couldn't be seen as being any different from the other children. Suddenly the whole place was released from the need to be cool.*

PENNY WILSON

**Penny Wilson**

# PLAYWORKERS AND THE ADVENTURE PLAY MOVEMENT

**Penny Wilson has been a playworker since the mid-1980s. For a large part of that time she worked at Chelsea Adventure Playground, an inclusive site where disabled children and their peers could play together. She is now employed as the Inclusion Worker at the Play Association Tower Hamlets, (PATH) in the east end of London where she lives. She also writes about play and provides playwork training. www.theinternaionale.net/playstories.**

It was an uncharacteristically sunny day in London just before I left in May.

I sat in the garden enjoying the bright warmth and catching glimpses of my daughter Charlie and her friend Eire, whom she had met at the local climbing wall, through the pinkwhite blossom and the very green, still, spring leaves. The blackbirds were showing off again.

The girls were scrambling up and down her climbing frame and throwing each other jokes, weaving a living den from tendrils of overgrown Russian vine. They were covered in mud from their games with the rainwater barrel, watering her newly planted garden.

They had twigs and blossoms tangled in their hair, and they were wearing a curious mixture of everyday and dressing up clothes.

They stopped to consult swiftly, then chargd down the garden path towards the house, pausing only to lift a paving slab so that Charlie could introduce Eire to her pet centipede. Then on they scibbled.

Then off galumphing up the stairs.

This is all very enchanting. However, I am sharing this snippet of domesticity with you because as a playworker I look at this story with a particular methodology in mind.

The first is that story telling allows us faithfully to represent the playing of children. We can mirror their experiences with our words.

The second is that these girls were playing in an "enriched" and "holding" play environment. This situation allows time and space for the children to play freely and safely in an environment that is filled with a broad range of opportunities for many different play types (Hughes & Winnicott).

The third is the presence of a playful adult who attends the playing but does not "adulterate" it by interrupting with an adult agenda (Sturrock).

The fourth is that within this short story are represented about 13 examples of different play types. I am referring here to the 16 Playtypes identified by Bob Hughes from current scientific research in his Taxonomy.

For almost all of my working life, I have been a senior playworker on an adventure playground in London. Where I work is inclusive, welcoming children with a wide range of disabilities and their peers.

It is not, financially, a wealthy site. What we do have is sole use of a fenced area with a natural environment and a building to play inside. We have children and a staff team. And we have lots of "loose parts" (Nicholson). These are things that can be anything. Some are toys, but mostly we have stones and hunks of wood and endless yards of fabric, rope, tires, old kitchen equipment, leaves, dressing up clothes, paint, cooking stuff, Christmas decorations, and glitter. I am never quite sure if I should count sand and water in this list, but for our purposes here, I will. Most of this equipment has been scrounged, found or bought cheaply.

I have never had a day there that has not contained at least one miracle. Some moment was revealing, or a child or group of children showed their genius for play.

Inspectors sometimes come to visit and ask to see our timetable of activities. We don't have any such thing. It is laughable to think that we should. We work much harder than that.

How could I timetable Jan's Moment of Wonder?

Jan is on the Autistic spectrum. He doesn't use speech and, because of various medical and personal factors, we have Risk Assessed him as needing the support of a one-to-one worker so that he can play in safety.

On this playground, like many others in the UK, parents leave their children at the playground, in the care of the playworkers for a whole day.

If you consider the times of your own rich playing, then I am sure that you will not associate an adult as being a part of that play. As workers with Jan and any other child, the playworker in the play environment must not adulterate the playframe of the child.

Children's play is "behaviour that is Freely Chosen, Personally Motivated and Intrinsically Directed" (Playwork Principals 2005 with reference to many sources). This small phrase describing play can sound so glib and easy on the ear. But every time I unpick it, its meaning, the depth of what it captures, catches my breath.

So, when we meet Jan in play, we use what he does, what we observe of him, his interests and passions, as a starting point for coaxing him into a world of free play. Like so many disabled children, Jan didn't have the chance to direct his own playing before he came to our site.

He was play deprived.

So, we mirror him. We don't rush up to him and try to become his friend. Our own desire to be popular is an adulteration of the agenda. However, by mirroring his playing, we can get a sense of what he is getting from it. Some of the characteristics familiar to people who play with children with Autism, such as scrabbling, rocking, clapping and hand flickering, make sense when you try them out for yourself. Through joining him in his activities we can show him that his playing is important: we validate it and show that we are interested in it too.

We are not trying to Normalise him.

Inevitably, the child will begin to meet us through the triangulation of the activity, and the agenda is set. "Here, you can play and we value your playing." (Our one playground rule is, "play as you want to here, but try not to hurt yourself or anyone else." This is an Infinite Rule. It is endlessly adaptable and flexible.)

Jan's Wonder happened on a bright London day like the one in the garden story about my daughter that I started with. I was working with him and observing him, very closely, from as far away as possible. At a certain point, he stopped in his tracks and backed up a pace or two. He then began an uncharacteristic rocking movement, which he kept up for ages, rocking forward and back. I was curious to see what he was doing and stepped a little closer, mirroring his action, stance and movement. I understood and crept away again to leave him in peace.

Now, in many settings an Autistic child rocking back and forth would have been either ignored or interrupted by staff hustling the child away because the child was being obsessive (and the adults were indulging in adulteration).

But my wonderful colleagues, one by one, noticed Jan's movement, thought it curious, mirrored it, understood, smiled to themselves and walked away.

Jan had shown us all his Wonder: he walked past a tree and caught the sun bursting around the trunk. He had been so amazed and struck by the splendour of what he saw that he decided, without a second thought, to go back and see it again and again and again.

In our meeting, our reflective practice, at the end of the day, we talked about how many of us had shared this beauty because of him. We agreed that we would probably continue to do this throughout the rest of our lives.

Joan visited an adventure playground in London with me last year.

Again the sun was brilliant. A pool of water had been put out, ready for the children to play with. Beside it was a tub of coloured chunky chalks. A boy scampered in and saw the tub of chalks and upended it into the water, because he knows it is okay to do that here. I could feel Joan watching. As a teacher she felt compelled to interrupt this process —but she acts as a playworker and doesn't adulterate.

The child kneels and watches the bubbles plip from the sticks of chalk. A playworker kneels next to him and describes in words which the child cannot voice, the things they are watching together: the bubbles rising, the chalks changing colour and drifting lazily to the bottom of the pool. They are transfixed. Then suddenly, the game is done, and the boy has a new drive. He takes the tub of water and turns into the sun; moving away from the people around, he throws the water into the light. He has invented water fireworks. I copy him and tell about the infinite patterns and rainbows and the slow speediness of the water as it falls through the sparkles and shards of light, about the colours that are created and the shapes I can see, because of him.

What would have happened if the child had been prevented, by a Joan from a parallel universe, from tipping the chalk into the water?

Well, nothing.

What if this happens every time a child has a quirky play instinct?

Again, nothing.

Our shared world would never have had the still magic of bubbling, floating, colour changing chalks and water fireworks.

"So what?" You may ask.

But ask rather, "What if?" and "Why not?"

The next is a sad story, but it always feels very important to me to emphasise that play is not only fun. It does serious work in the most beautiful and poetic way. A child was referred to us by Social Services. He was profoundly deaf. He had been taken away from the family home, which was a Muslim one, and placed with a foster carer who was Christian. He was given no sign language interpreter to explain what was happening or why or for how long he would be in this caring but alien environment. He was in deep distress.

After a few weeks he came to trust our faltering sign language and the ethos of the playground. He understood that this place was for him to do what he needed to. It was the middle of winter. He went outside, stood in the centre of our dry splash pool, and poured bucket after bucket load of dry, pure powder paint over his head. Layer after layer of vibrant colour tumbled over him, sometimes mushing into mud colours, sometimes a pure vibrant confusion of colour. Which of us could find a way so perfectly to express the multiple layers of desperate confusion and love that this child was experiencing?

These amazing things are happening at eighty adventure playgrounds in London and many more throughout the UK, and wherever else children are allowed to play freely.

The adventure play movement grew from the work of Lady Allen of Hurtwood who, inspired by the work of the Danish architect Sorensen, made up her mind to create a movement of adventure playgrounds on the bombsites of the UK after World War II. These spaces were dedicated solely to the free playing of children and overseen by "Wardens." Children could play in sand and mud and water; they could make gardens and dig caves and use wood and tools to make dens and climbing structures. They built fires and cooked their food. The Wardens observed and reflected on the playing of the children. They worked out ways to protect and enhance these environments and quickly came to understand that the playgrounds were community hubs.

From the sharing of this work, the profession of Playwork grew. As Wardens talked together, they realised that the playing that they saw was universal and that their responses were universal too. They realised that the same sort of play is vi-

tal in the lives of all children. Lady Allen quickly realised that this applied to disabled children as well, and established a string of playgrounds designed to meet their needs, allowing them to play alongside their peers.

And now?

In the UK, we can study play at Vocational, Degree and Masters levels. We have an established profession of people who rejoice in relinquishing power to children and who celebrate quirkiness. We are there for the children, but we do not dominate their play. We support and encourage it, and always we learn from it.

A playworker friend of mine told me about a session around a campfire. One of the kids present was a bit of a handful; he has ADHD. But as he sat and watched the fire, he became calm. He said to my friend, "Mo, when I grow up, I want to be a flame."

When I watch a playground of children at work, I am aware of the process, not the product. I see a complexity and an intricacy and a beauty that is like a dance, but more than that.

I see the internal worlds of so many people, freed up and coming out to play together in a dedicated space in the external world. It is what Winnicott describes as the ideal way of living.

Coming at the world creatively.

Constantly seeing the world anew.

A lifetime burning in every moment.

## Ronald Fleming

# A CHILDHOOD SHAPED BY
# A GHOST TOWN

**Ronald Lee Fleming played a pioneering role in the Main Street Revitalization Movement and has subsequently done innovative urban design work on placemaking. His most recent book *The Art of Placemaking: Interpreting Community Through Public Art and Design* was published by Merrell Publishers in 2007.**

When considering life choices we have made, it sometimes takes the perspective of years to understand what choices we command and what command us.

I've spent a professional career working on the main streets of old towns and doing "placemaking," projects recovering the memory of mutual associations with the fabric of towns. Was I predestined to go into planning because I had constructed my "ghost town" on land next to our house in Los Angeles County?

As a young boy, I spent ten years directing other boys in my neighborhood in the fabrication of a wooden town based on ghost towns seen with my parents. Starting with a fascination for artifacts like travel post cards in my grandmother's beach house basement, my imaginative world expanded to the discovery of buildings and places. When I was about five or six, we went to Knott's Berry Farm in Anaheim. This early recreation park south east of Los Angeles included a restaurant, berry fields and a re-created mining town that the Knott family had constructed on their farm land. That mining ghost town now surrounded by urban development had an impact on Walt Disney, as well as on me, his Disneyland reducing to 5/8 scale its main street facades. The chicken dinners and the raspberry jam at Knott's Berry Farm were always part of this adventure, my own Proustian madeleine cookie.

Warm biscuits with that jam recall for me this reconstructed town where one could buy a sarsaparilla drink, look at the stern wooden visage of a dime store Indian, peer into a mine shaft, and hear honky tonk music from the swinging doors of an old time saloon. This experience encouraged me to badger my parents into going out to see authentic towns: Ransburg, and Ryolite, Bodie, and Calico, Virginia City and the mother lode towns on the 49er highway, a lexicon of places that I had committed to memory by the time I was ten.

They helped me build my own small wooden town on the land that we owned adjacent to our house on a hillside in Los Angeles County. I think it was one of the great acts of generosity in my childhood that my parents never mentioned the water bill! This bone dry land next to our house kept a stream going for years from a faucet at the top of the property. From the street,

the land sloped up across a small patch of ivy, edged at the top with a row of oleander bushes, which usually protected the neighbors from the perennial construction site of my town. Still the fire department usually came once a year to see if some conflagration could sweep through the wooden buildings and boardwalks, the hotel with a second story where we sometimes slept, the sheriff's office, the general store, the bridges over the stream winding down from the top of the property through beds of iris. In the front of the town, a vegetable garden sprouted large stalks of corn in the summer months. At the top was a large patch, where we could pick our own berries.

The town was really an endless source of amusement. At the "hangman hotel" we had a carved wooden figure of a man that hung by a noose from the front door. My father had given us good lumber for the sheriff's office and the hotel, and he had helped in the construction of these two buildings. I was never that handy at construction but had ideas about how it should be done. Additional lumber was salvaged from the packing crates at the printing company belonging to the father a school chum. In Tom Sawyer fashion I was able to cajole a handful of boys to help me.

I don't remember going often to playgrounds or doing organized sports. In a sense we invented with the ghost town what Lady Allen of Hurtwood, the English planner after WWII, had described as an "adventure playground." Here in California we children had a chance to define one ourselves. There wasn't a grid; there wasn't an accepted way of doing things. Everything evolved from the collective imagination of children who brought a complete town into being. How fulfilling it was not to be defined by adults or by their playground equipment. It changed the very nature of games. Everyone could participate; it wasn't competitive except in the sense that one could be recognized for the power of a good idea.

Of course, there were endless games of cowboys and Indians in this town. We had wonderful cap guns then, probably banned today as too realistic and a threat to society. And we created "headstones," not actually stones but wooden boards we painted with epitaphs. It was our own "boot hill," and although no bodies were buried there, the memories remain anchored by these artifacts.

Our world survived intact until the bulldozers came when I was fifteen.

So yes, I had the memories of invention, construction, and finally demolition when communities were displaced by urban renewal as bulldozers swept away the elaborate wooden gingerbread houses on Bunker Hill in downtown Los Angeles, which my father had taken me to see.

Indeed, all these memories came back with a rush when I finally understood that there was such a thing as a school with a graduate degree in planning! Working in old towns and pioneering main street projects in New England during the early years of my career were the fulfillment of a Proustian memory of the raspberry jam and biscuits at Knott's Berry Farm where a recreated mining town linked me to the American West.

**Jean Vortkamp**

## FRONT PORCH

### A Youth Program Based Solely on Relationships

**Jean Vortkamp lives in Detroit. She is the director of the organization with constant help from her sister, Mary Jo Vortkamp, and her neighbor, Karen Horn, and all the neighborhood kids.**

The Front Porch's mission is to provide educational and recreational opportunities to youth according to their interests and initiatives. We started as a part of a block club in 1995 with one volunteer, five kids, some books and origami. Now there is a group of over 50 kids ranging in age from five to eighteen, ten volunteers, and four teen employees. The Front Porch extends to all the kids' friends and relatives who visit the neighborhood. There are more and more kids all the time. Sometimes they return from down south—most kids in Detroit have relatives from Mississippi, Georgia and North Carolina. They return from the west side of Detroit. They visit from the suburbs. Our only wish would be to have an excellent school so the kids in our neighborhood could get the education they have a right to. Our most successful programming takes place on the porch. For special events, classes, and regularly scheduled programming, we use the Kelly-Morang Senior Center, and in the summer we have used the City of Detroit Heilmann Recreation Center.

We believe that if children and youth have a safe, informal place where they are free to express their opinions and explore their talents and skills supported by adults and to meet other kids, then we should see a change in the attitude of the children and eventually the whole neighborhood. It should not be just a place to live, but an interdependent place in which to grow, communicate, learn and explore: a safe place from which to begin a life not bounded by a neighborhood, but rather a life rooted in a place that is a springboard to the world.

My front porch is in a brick-house neighborhood on the eastside of Detroit. We are not a very air-conditioned neighborhood. People sit on their porches to cool down. The porch on my house is a six foot square slab of concrete on bricks. It is set back into the house, is open, and the sun beats down mercilessly in the afternoon. To the right, there are four houses. Next door is a vacant house owned by an unknown bank. There is another house, and then the corner house where stuffed animals are nailed to a tree in memorial for a teenager from a different neighborhood who died in the alley. At the end of the street is a busy intersection one can plainly see. This is the place

that became a support for many neighborhood kids. We are just sitting on the porch—sometimes with more funding than others, sometimes in the midst of gunshots, and sometimes in the midst of beautiful breezy days perfect for a game of tag.

I grew up in this neighborhood when it was the murder capital of the world. It was the neighborhood with White Boy Rick and Young Boys Incorporated. It's the neighborhood where the rich kids from Grosse Pointe would get houses to sell drugs out of the sight of their wealthy parents. I grew up unaware of these facts, sheltered in private school, backyards and after school activities. It was the time when drugs were more secretive. I grew up playing from dawn to dusk in a school where play was important for classtime, recess and lunch. My early years were spent in sandboxes making mud muffins, in refrigerator box houses and organizing the neighborhood to put on plays. All I ever wanted was to play.

When I was in college, I lived in the same house. I went away to university in Europe for a semester. I lived in a quiet neighborhood in Prague near the castle there. I returned home suddenly aware of constant gunshots. I was taking a peace studies class and began to think about non-violence and became aware that although violence was normal to me in the past, I had to make myself aware that it was unacceptable. The violence was getting worse every day. We had run-bys—13 or 14 year olds shooting the street up in broad daylight. There were constant drive-bys which made the arrangement of a couch in front of the front window in the house unacceptable home décor. Homemade bombs were always a surprise. SWAT teams in the bushes crushed carefully planted flowers. Crack was sold like Avon. Elementary kids brought guns to school.

I wanted to see where the gun shots were coming from. Who were these out of control cowboys of Detroit? I began to do my university homework on the porch. There I found children who wanted something—anything—to do. It was extremely disturbing to see the backdrop of my neighborhood, a place full of hiding spots and sidewalk squares for four-square, becoming a place where children didn't know how to play. The girls spent their free time talking about each other and the boys would fight and play at being their gang brothers. The local recreation center was a mile and a half away, through a worse neighborhood. It hadn't been fixed up for decades. They had begun a gym, but someone managed to steal the construction money when I was a kid. I didn't know how to get the kids there anyway.

We always had a neighborhood association, AWARE, in my area. Drugs were drowning us:neighbors were losing their sense of safety. They were suffering crimes like being mugged on the way between their car and house. The neighborhood association would meet in a local church basement, each of us wondering if our possessions would still be in our houses when we returned. The situation of the neighborhood changed very little from the meetings. I realized that the major changes were in the forming of relationships and having a sense of power. It doesn't matter if a neighborhood group accomplishes anything in the physical world, as long as people feel they have a place to be heard and listened to.

My mom, a longtime supporter of the neighborhood association, always lent out the bike pump to the neighborhood kids. I started to call block club meetings with the neighbors. We came, we met. Less and less adults would come, but children remained. Maybe it was just for the cookies. I started to ask them what they wanted. With a few of the neighbors and my mom and sister, we began to give them things to do. My sister, the librarian, would bring them books. My mom and my neighbors would give me advice. Grandma Belva had severe diabetes but would give me craft suggestions. Next door, Grandma Gene would give me advice on dealing with parents and find games at garage sales for the kids. Another friend's Grandma Kubika would give me advice about dealing with the adults in the community. Her usual pep speech would begin with "To hell with them."

I would bring out crafts and games for the kids on the porch. For two years, we would do anything with them that was available. Most of our materials were recycled, from garage sales, or stuff from my or the neighbors' attics. We began to play, to create a safe place in the midst of a war.

The kids weren't sure how to play. They had been focused on acting like the older siblings who babysat them. By getting them away from their older siblings, they would be free to act like kids again, and the older siblings got respite from being in charge. We made cupcakes on the porch, snowmen, papier-mache shoes, masks, and built houses from anything.

The leader of our local community group suggested I ask to use the local senior center in the evening. It was a five block walk from the porch. It's a small storefront. It seats about 30 people, with a little kitchen in the back. The basement leaks and smells horrible when it rains. The tables are rickety and many of the chairs are broken. I attended an endless set of meetings there where they would grill me about what I planned to do with children there. In the meantime, we used the library, but couldn't get there too often as it was over a mile away. At the library, the kids did treasure hunts through the stacks and raced around the world in the atlases using latitude and longitude clues. I had them meet any people from other countries I knew. I wanted them to know the world was bigger than our street. I wanted them to know that living under constant threat of being killed is not normal or acceptable. We often had to end games of Uno or tag early because a fight was about to erupt or cars were circling the block ready to take aim. Sometimes we would see federal agents sitting in their cars on the block—old white men just sitting around in cars on our street—as if that was undercover!

I took the kids to the local refugee shelter. I thought they would find a sort of kinship with those kids and provide them some welcome company. I just knew that kids who live in wars of any kind still needed to play. I had worked with a social worker who worked with refugees, Nene, who explained that even in the midst of a war, where families have little food, they can still celebrate a birthday—even if the only gift is a pencil. Kids need their childhood regardless of the nonsense grownups are engaged in.

I was also struck by a concentration camp I visited just outside Prague, where an art teacher and several children were among the prisoners. He taught them art as they waited to die. I thought about him sometimes when I was rushing the kids home, pretending they were in trouble, when really I was warned that there was about to be a shooting. I would think, "If he could do that knowing he was going to die, I can be strong enough to fake this through."

Fortunately for our finances, I had taken a culture class at a local nonprofit, New Detroit, recommended by a board member. When the senior center wanted us to have insurance before we used their facility, I asked at New Detroit and luckily a director there wrote us a check for our first insurance. We would not be here today without that. There is no funder for just insurance. The senior center also told us we had to be a 501(c)3. I took a class at the Volunteer Accounting organization. They gave us the forms and told us what to do. A friend donated the money for filing and I filled it in. A few months later, we were a 501(c)3. From there I wrote for mini-grants.

At the senior center, we made messes and irritated the senior center director (carpets and large groups of children never mix). Fortunately, the director of the whole center was friends with the mother of a neighbor. He knew the nightmare stories of our block and protected us from being kicked out. The center offered to write a Neighborhood Opportunity Fund grant for us. They wrote the grant for us and were our fiduciary. It took about three years to get the first contract through. We had no money to start the reimbursement with, so they fronted it for us. The money comes painfully slowly through the City, so we are all on the edge of collapse financially. This year, a worker in the department told us we never had a contract. The paperwork for reimbursement sat for a year without being processed. Fortunately the community center had a huge budget and can absorb these shocks. If we were alone, we would have sunk. One of our donors donated mainly because she saw us working this process and said she had seen so many nonprofits collapse from "molasses funding."

The library helped us tremendously. My sister the librarian had lived on the same block and has helped from the beginning. Through her aid, the library gave us meeting space. Their books supplied us with activity ideas and we participate in the summer reading club. We couldn't get to the library to participate, so she brought us books and got the kids on the street to the reading race every summer, ending in a party and prizes. The kids race to see who reads the most books over the summer. We have some tubs full of donated books sorted by age we pull out. They read the book and can either write about the books or answer three questions about the content.

At the center, we hosted photography and dance lessons through a program at Wayne State University—Arts in the Neighborhood. The program brought a bunch of youth serving nonprofits in Detroit together and asked them what they wanted to help their groups. They decided on dance and photography lessons. The teachers were undergraduate students. The university supplied the teachers, supplies and the training for the teachers. They paid one person at each nonprofit to be a liaison for the teachers. I got involved because I went to Wayne State and a professor told me about it. We met around the city, so I got a chance to see how other nonprofits worked.

One of our first main projects was a neighborhood garden. I had taken a neighborhood mediation class and met an urban gardener there, Gerald Hairston. My grandmother lived one street over and always had an urban garden. Our family always had something growing. The whole eastside of Detroit is filled with backyard gardens. He suggested I make a garden with the kids. I found the closest empty lot on a safe street. (It was at least safe until dusk.) At the neighborhood association meeting, a woman suggested I speak to a particular family on that street. I went and knocked on their door and met LaTanya and her wonderful family. They let us use their water and were interested in the project. Her kids and some other kids down the block started it. Eventually, most of the kids on that block worked in that garden. We started with a three sisters garden, a Native American tradition with corn, beans and squash. Eventually, the kids did more and more of the planning for the garden. We got compost, plants and seeds with help from City's Farm-a-Lot program. We begged lots of donations.

Over the years it got better and better. Each year ended with a garden party. In the third year of the garden, Tyree, one of the kids from next door, wrote a youth grant to the Community Foundation. We got the grant and put in fruit trees, a pond and lots of roses. The garden was never perfect. We had only a few adult volunteers. One neighbor would complain it was a mess. Kids came and went as they pleased in it. We had no money for a good fence: we didn't own the land and couldn't. It was owned by a man who wanted to sell it to us, but the city still had back taxes on the land owed from when a house was there. The house was being refurbished when the city demolished it. He was unable to clear the taxes.

At the garden one mom came down to see what her daughter had been working in. Her name was Ms. Karen, and she began to help us with the garden. LaTanya was sick and moved. We had been getting water from the neighbors on the other side and paid them. Then they cut off the water. The neighbors further down let us use their water. We used wagons and coolers on wheels. This infuriated the mean man next door, whose children worked on it quite often, and he ripped it apart in the middle of the night.

That ended the garden, much to the pain of the many children and adults who worked on it. I still remember two of the most involved kids sneaking over there, rescuing some vegetables for a final garden meal and picking the last surviving flowers. There was no way to re-establish the garden there with him living next door.

We moved the garden to the lady across the street's house on my block. Her name was Hope. We put raised beds there and grew strawberries and vegetables. We had a picnic. There were a lot less kids, but at least it kept going. Some of the older kids built a sandbox for Hope's son. He loved the garden.

Then she moved and the garden went on my front lawn. We have a few boxes there, a few boxes in Ms. Karen's backyard, a few in Ms. Gene's backyard and some plants in the back-yards of the kids who wanted them. We also planned and planted a garden at the conserva-tory on Belle Isle last year. The Belle Isle Bo-tanical Society decided it was not neat enough for their project. They told us our kids could plant it, but that they would name it and plan it. Gardening should be like play for kids (and for adults).

Each year we got a pet. We began with three ducklings, Matt, Jack, and Pat from the 4H program. The kids put them in the baby swimming pool in front of the house. Grand-ma Ruby down the street would come with her granddaughter twins. The little boys held the ducklings and took care of them. The ducks went to live at the farm program at the school for pregnant girls (Catherine Ferguson Academy) in Detroit. Then we got butterflies and raised them. The kids were always amazed to see them come out of their shells. Then we got a grey rabbit, Forever, who lived for three years. We also have a worm bin which the kids watch like they watch TV. At the pond at the garden we had frogs and fish, which were promptly stolen within days of their entry.

Through a connection from the university, I became involved in High/Scope's program and was educated about adolescents. I remem-ber one trainer saying that he had never seen a youth program based solely on relationships before.

At the community center, a woman from the advisory board, Ora Brown Davis, tried to convince us to bring the kids to Heilmann, the neighborhood recreation center. Eventu-ally, we started to go there. At first, we rode bikes—the neighborhood near the recreation center had gotten better since the Porch be-gan. Then we began to have a formal sum-mer program where we walked up there and then got a van ride home. The pool was still nice even though the showers were rusted and slippery. The director kindly let us use the one activity room the center had, painted peeling prison blue.

Sometimes the workers hid the fans from us during scorching Detroit summers. We stopped using the room and just had classes outside on the lawn. We brought blankets

In, Around and After School

# Hugh McDiarmid and Brad Garmon

# SAFE ROUTES TO DETROIT SCHOOLS

A Photo Essay

**Hugh McDiarmid and Brad Garmon work for the Michigan Environmental Council, a coalition of 75 environmental, public health, and faith-based groups dedicated to preserving and protecting the state's natural resources and the economic and health benefits that flow from them.**

Sometimes all children need to engage their imaginations, their muscles and their freedom is simply to get rid of the manmade barriers that prevent them from doing so.

That is the goal of an international movement designed to make it safe and convenient for children to walk or bike to school. An old-fashioned concept? Sure. But it comes in an era where numerous obstacles stand in the way. Crime, blight, distance, loose dogs, multi-lane thoroughfares, remote cul-de-sac and lack of paths or sidewalks are among the reasons why parents protect their kids from the pitfalls of post-sprawl pedestrianism by driving them or busing them.

Thirty years ago, about two-thirds of children walked or biked to school, giving them freedom, exercise, and a connection with their neighborhood nooks and crannies. Today, only

13 percent of kids walk or bike to class according to the Centers for Disease Control.

The Safe Routes to School initiative has enjoyed success in Michigan. In Detroit, community involvement, student buy-in, technological wizardry, generous doses of common sense and progressive thinking have helped engage students to identify and demolish the hazards that prevent them from frequently walking and biking to classes.

The results have been similarly encouraging across the country, where the project has been molded to fit the unique needs and challenges of each community. Why bother?

In a broad sense, a community engaged in scrutinizing walking routes to schools with an eye toward identifying and eliminating hazards makes for better neighborhoods, provides role models for children and strengthens the spirit vital to the fabric of society.

And for the children, the payoffs are myriad. Walking is an easy way to get the regular physical exercise that is essential for good health and a chance for relaxed and spontaneous social interaction. The children also are empowered as part of a community team—identifying problems along their walking routes and then watching them be resolved by adults and authority figures who respond to their concerns.

"It's the perfect type of project for kids to learn something and connect with their community," said David Martin, a research professor at Wayne State University who has helped implement the Safe Routes program in several Detroit neighborhoods.

That community connection is particularly needed in Detroit, where students must face multiple obstacles to success including high unemployment, low incomes, a troubling crime rate and an aging infrastructure.

In a city once supported by a tax base of 2 million residents, Detroit's population has declined to 850,000 leaving vast stretches of abandoned and burned-out homes that are the province of squatters, drug dealers and transients whom children must navigate on their way to and from school. What's more, a cash-starved city government is often unable to provide basic safety measures like working street lights, prompt police response, and timely demolition of condemned buildings.

So the Safe Routes program in Detroit fills a desperate need. But beyond safety, there is also the incalculable benefit that the outdoors has on youngsters who may often spend most of their free hours indoors, hostages to fear or slaves to electronic games. As Richard Louv, author of *Last Child in the Woods*, explained: "At the very moment we are breaking the bond between the young and the natural world, a growing body of research links our mental, spiritual and physical health directly to our association with nature." Louv's book explores scientific links between healthy outdoors experiences and lower rates of childhood depression, asthma, attention deficit disorder and other problems that are prevalent in urban America.

In Detroit, programs are tailored to fit community needs and expectations, typically incorporating global positioning technology, public records databases and good old-fashioned street smarts.

Using geographic information systems and portable computers, 9th graders at Detroit's Southeastern High School have been locating, mapping and publicizing unsafe conditions in their neighborhoods in a project supported by the Southeastern Village community group and the Detroit Public Schools.

Wayne State University researchers trained students to use the mapping software to pinpoint conditions of concern in their neighborhoods—abandoned homes, trash-strewn lots, and suspicious persons.

Digital photographs accompany the mapping, which is combined with property records databases that identified the owners of suspect homes and lots. The students and community groups lobbied city leaders for solutions with success.

"The kids speaking out has more of an impact in getting junk cars hauled away and homes boarded up than the usual community activists who are speaking about the problem day after day," said Martin. "They gave presentations, Power Point presentations they developed, to mayoral appointees and department heads. We have some very powerful before and after evidence of what was accomplished."

The computer knowledge and civic activism experiences are skills students can use immediately on resumes. "It's powerful and very persuasive information," said Martin. Students reported feeling safer walking to schools and better about their neighborhoods, said Lynn Smith, director of the nonprofit Southeastern Village community group, which worked with the students.

"It's not only safety and security, but the look of the area," said Smith. "It's improved the attitudes of the children and the look of the community. Their whole outlook has been affected."

That makes Kamille Tynes feel good. The Southeast High student has encountered aggressive dogs, drug dealers and streets dim from lack of streetlight replacement. Helping map problem areas in 2005/2006 as part of the Safe Routes project has empowered her, and she's re-enlisted in the program for her junior year in 2006-2007.

"There are groups of guys selling dope and abandoned houses and it makes it very uncomfortable," she said. "But helping get the abandoned houses boarded up has really made me feel like I accomplished something and helped Detroit." School is "a second home" for lots of troubled teens, said Tynes. Getting there shouldn't be stressful, especially when "things might be crazy at home, and they want to go to school where they can relax."

She said the neighborhoods also are safer for younger children who like to roam the nooks and crannies of alleys, backyards and vacant lots: "Even though maybe they're told they're not supposed to, they'll go out in a hot second and explore," she said. "It's just their nature." In 2005-2006, Smith's group reported 29 abandoned homes that had been boarded up, several abandoned cars towed and numerous vacant lots cleaned up as a direct result of the students' activism. "The city director of building and safety said the students' work would have taken his staff weeks to do," she said. "The kids were really excited to learn that the city was acting on their findings."

Several other Detroit neighborhoods have used the Safe Routes concept, including Spain Middle School students who integrated a mapping project into their technology and social studies curricula. "This gives the students an awareness of their community and their surroundings and how they can improve it and be involved," a computer technology teacher at Spain told *Education World Magazine* in May, 2006.

The Wayne County prosecutor's office began targeting the area for housing code enforcement, and students presented their information to the Detroit City Council. The resulting demolitions decreased the number of abandoned homes in one neighborhood by more than 50 percent, according to *Education World*.

The Safe Routes program defies any attempt at a one-size-fits-all description because of the vast difference among the communities where it has been implemented. Detroit's example—a struggling urban school district beset by poverty, abandoned properties and many families who don't own automobiles—is aimed toward making students safe. In other, more affluent areas, the goal has been a reduction in the reliance on personal vehicles to transport children to classes. The trend toward building new mega-schools among farm fields on the far outer fringes of town often leaves children with only one option for getting to class: a daily car commute that consumes valuable time and resources for parents and society.

Marin County, California, with one of the highest per-capita incomes in the U.S., implemented the first Safe Routes program in the nation in 2000. It is focused on reducing congestion around schools by encouraging walking and biking. The county reports a 64 percent increase in the number of kids walking to school and a 114 percent hike in the number using bicycles. The number of kids arriving at school singly by private vehicle decreased by 39 percent.

The decrease in vehicle traffic has saved 2.6 million vehicle miles, according to the county's program evaluation. That reduction saves fuel and eliminated 11.7 tons of tailpipe pollution that otherwise would have contributed to myriad childhood health problems like asthma and the worldwide climate change woes.

Safe Routes has enjoyed similar success across the nation, bolstered by $612 million in federal transportation money approved in 2005 for the program. At least $1 million is allocated per year to each of the 50 states over a five-year period. In addition to mapping and neighborhood initiatives, the money is being used to construct new bike lanes, paths and sidewalks as well as education and promotional campaigns. To learn how to get a Safe Routes to School Program started, visit www.saferoutesinfo.org.

valiant heroes, you don't try to change the rules right away, something my parents could never have taught me.

Our way of life is undergoing rapid change. Globalization, mass communication, international migration, world trade, sophisticated mass-produced weaponry, and terrorism have changed the way we reflect upon ourselves, our lives, and needs. Along with everything else, the world of children has become unsettled. Unsupervised play in parks and cul-de-sacs is a thing of the past. Fear of the "predators" seen on TV has made parents very vigilant. The media's grisly focus makes us cope with imagined dangers by closely supervising our children and their play. Close monitoring of play is often accompanied by heightened adult intervention. Conflict during play, a normative behavior for young children, has come under intense scrutiny. The result, as I have witnessed in my classroom, is that children become ignorant of the real consequences of fighting with friends since all they often experience is scripted adult intervention. As a researcher and a teacher I am intrigued by children's conflict during play, just as much as I am by their ability to quickly seek out friends and become one with the culture of a classroom, a culture in constant flux. The more the children get to know each other, the more complex their play becomes and conflict starts taking on a new meaning. The children constantly negotiate their personal understand-

ing of each other. Some of these understandings appear to have been arrived at through conflict. A heated dispute consisting of grabbing and snatching for an orange marker, for example, results in a later declaration that, "We are friends and her favorite color is orange too."

Conflicts are a common occurrence, whether in the social or the mental realm. Where there is interaction, disagreements and opposition are inevitable. Opposition establishes a relationship between combatants, which in turn directs interaction (Ross & Conant, 1992). Looked at from this perspective, conflict creates its own social process and has implications for the social order of the entire classroom culture that extends beyond the boundaries of any particular dispute. Conflict, then, holds great potential for not only individual development but also for the organization of relationships and social structures.

Much has been said about using the "teaching moments" that arise from conflict between children. In contrast, far less has been said about letting conflicts become "learning moments" for children. As a teacher I observed that play continued successfully when there was a certain mutuality of purpose between/amongst participants. This mutuality of purpose refers to the notion of intersubjectivity or shared understanding between participants (Rogoff, 1990). Piaget and Vygotsky hypothesize that intersubjectivity in play emerges in the third year of life when solitary play gives way to social play and then on increases with age. Like them, I believe that children achieve intersubjectivity through negotiation of personal understanding of each other. Much of the understanding is arrived at through conflict during play.

Increasingly, adults resolve conflict between children. This intervention, I believe, acts as an impediment to the forming of intersubjectivity between the children. Just by their presence and constant modeling, adults continually pass on values to children. Like language skills, morals, social values, and ethics are learnt first as dichotomous conceptions of "good" and "bad," "right" and "wrong," "appropriate" and "inappropriate." Once these become familiar, children experiment with the depth and range of all that lies between in order to come to an intrinsic understanding. An adult's mere presence should provide sufficient social structure and stability for the children to be able to resolve conflict in a manner that promotes personal understanding of each other by trying and testing the boundaries and limits of new relationships during play. The play environment in all its variety presents just such an opportunity because play provides the ambiguity (Sutton-Smith, 1997) that conflicts and, thus, understandings thrive on. Play is crucial to the children's understanding of the larger culture because it exhibits social structures quite similar to those found in other aspects of life (Henricks, 2006).

The following vignette shows how even a three year old is capable of negotiating an understanding on her own terms.

Erika, a three year old, was pushed away roughly by James, a four year old, when she came up to where he was playing with toy farm animals. Student teachers rushed to intercede and the two were asked to articulate their feelings and asked to "use their words" in future. The episode ended with James apologizing to Erika who replied, "Oh! Alright!" and walked away. Later, at snack time, Erika sat next to James and the two ate their snack in silence. Suddenly Erika turned towards James and the following conversation ensued.

Erika: "James, why you push me away?"(There is no anger expressed.)

James looks very confused, " I . . . . I . . . . Well. . . . I thought you wouldn't understand. . . . ..um I . . . . thought you wanted to spoil what I was doing."

Erika: " No, I just wanted to see."

James: "But I thought you would take something away."

Erika: "No. I just wanted to look."

James: " Okay I will let you look next time, okay?"

Erika: " Okay."

Still later that day, James says to a student

teacher, "That new girl Erika is my friend."

(FIELD NOTES, 9/12/00)

This episode illustrates the growing autonomy of the younger child in resolving a conflict which she initiated even after a teacher had apparently helped them negotiate. James agreed to let Erika play with him in the future not because a teacher told him it was right but because he had come to some sort of an understanding and appreciation of Erika's friendly overture. Such dialogue between peers encourages a mutual understanding that is invaluable in the building of relationships. There is the tantalizing possibility that Erika's and James's snack time exchange would have taken place earlier in the day had a teacher not intervened and instead let the children talk it over between themselves.

During my time as a teacher, I often heard children shouting the following out to each other:

a) " name of person I didn't like the way you grabbed that name of object from me. I don't like it when you do that."

b) "It was not nice to hit me. I don't want to play with you when you hit me."

Variation: "You are always hitting. I don't want to be your friend because you are always hitting me."

c) "It always makes me sad when you don't let me play in the loft/ sand table/porch with you. It makes me sad when you are nasty."

d) "You are mean. I don't like to play with you . . . you are always mean to all of us."

e) "name of person called me names. It is not nice to call names. Don't call me that again."

I also found that children's threats were more effective in eliciting the cooperation of their peers than punishments imposed by adults. A simple statement like, "I am not going to call you for my birthday," had children rush to cooperation, whereas a much more severe dictum by a teacher such as, "You may not play with that unless you share," was often followed by the child abandoning the toy, play, and peer altogether. I found that conflicts between friends were often moderated by their greater need to maintain continuity in their play but, by the same token, conflicts were also often moderated by the desire of one child to maintain the present interaction.

In the process of differing in opinion, ideology, view, or notions of how an activity should play out, children appeared to discover the potential for friendship. In cases where close ties had already been formed, it appeared that disputes gave the children an opportunity to work out the terms of their relationship. Children frequently showed by their actions that they were willing to change in order to acquire or maintain a relationship they thought was desirable.

## Notes

Henricks, T. (2006). *Play Reconsidered*. Chicago: University of Illinois Press.

Sutton-Smith, B. (1996). *The Ambiguity of Play*. Cambridge, Massachusetts: Harvard University Press.

Palmer, P. J. (1998). *The Courage to Teach: Exploring the Inner Landscape of a Teacher's Life*. San Francisco, California: Jossey-Bass.

Piaget, J. (1965). *The Moral Judgment of the Child*. New York: Free Press. (Originally published in 1932).

Rogoff, B. (1990). *Apprenticeship in Thinking: Cognitive Development in Social Context*. New York: Oxford University Press.

Ross, H. S., & Conant, C. L. (1992). "The social structure of early conflict: Interaction, relationships, and alliances." In C. U. Shantz & W. W. Hartup (Eds.), *Conflict in Child and Adolescent Development* (153-185). Cambridge: Cambridge University Press.

Vygotsky, L. S. (1962). *Thought and Language*. Cambridge, Massachusetts: M.I.T. Press.

WENDY RANSOM

## Frode Svane and Rhonda Clements

# CREATING NATURAL SPACES FOR MAKE-BELIEVE PLAY AND INCREASED PHYSICAL ACTIVITY

**Frode Svane is a Norwegian architect and educator. For further inspiration in planning children's outdoor environments, visit his website at "Children's Landscape": http://home.c2i.net/swan.**

**Rhonda Clements, Ed.D. is professor of education at Manhattanville College in Purchase, New York and author of nine books on children's play, games, and physical activity.**

**Box. . . .**

Shouts of "You've been captured!" sound out as four-year-old James bows his head in defeat, and is transported by two classmates to meet the fearless King and Queen who will determine his destiny. The children have named their leafy play space the "kidnapper-king-castle." James will join three other cohorts, also "kidnapped" and transported here. Within minutes James must make a decision to either concede to the King's and Queen's wishes, or to strategize a master escape plan with the other three young rebels. All of these decisions and actions must occur before the teacher signals the end of free play, when both sides instantly are transformed to their previous selves.

## Introduction

Most adults can recall and describe their own childhood adventures involving chasing, fleeing,

They also advocate planting semi-mature trees to give the play area visual form.

## Framing the Play Area

A fourth consideration focuses on using the natural landscape as a "frame" for make-believe play. The various topography of the natural landscape can inspire very vigorous actions among children. The anchor of a make-believe play episode involving chasing and fleeing might be as simple as a big root of an old tree, a stump, a log, or well placed boulders. "Caves," "grass tunnels" or "dens" can exist within bushes or a group of three or more trees. Even dead or "recycled trees" donated from the local Parks and Recreation Department offer children a place to balance, or sit on, as well as climb and jump over. Different terrain details such as knolls, depressions, holes, or distinct plateaus in a slope, give opportunities for crawling in snug places, jumping, bounding, and leaping, and also serve as "walls" or "space-dividers." Hillsides, mounds of dirt, stone structures, or any elevated structure such as a wooden stage or platform (12 to 18 inches) offer children opportunities to climb or scale different heights and levels with little fear of injury. Polish theatre director, Jerzy Grotowsky (1968), experimented with the concept of having his actors and spectators in different spatial positions and levels to each other, adding a third dimension to limited stage space. The same concept is true when young children recognize the feelings of power that differing heights gives to individuals.

## Securing and Selecting Natural Objects

Regretfully, many landowners still are in the process of cutting down all of the trees and bushes in many preschool centers and schoolyards, particularly in places where the shrubs might potentially cross the surrounding fences. For centuries, children within the USA have naturally flocked to patches of grass, or have had the opportunity to skip through grassy meadows. The need for parking lots, additional modular classrooms, local street violence, and decreases in school budgets for playground supervisors have played a major force in the disappearance of natural school yards.

Still, natural play environments are less expensive than large anchored conventional play structures. Native shrubs in the USA that combine the virtues of beauty and low maintenance in areas with limited rainfall include the olive, butterfly bush, potentilla, and barberry bush. Local nurseries can also recommend other common native shrubs (See Figure 6). Considerations for purchasing recommended shade trees for the area of the country where the school is located can be easily found by either contacting or visiting the website of The National Arbor Day Foundation. This comprehensive website contains a wealth of information and suggestions for selecting and purchasing the heartiest and most popular tree(s) for a specific area of the country.

Granted, local nurseries will be needed to transport and install large shade trees; however, many evergreen shrubs are sold for less than ten dollars for a one-gallon container. Sod costs average 50 to 75 cents per square foot that may seem expensive, until one compares the price of injuries on asphalt or the cost of tarred surfacing. When purchasing sod, the teacher leader is paying for an instant lawn area. Furthermore, the National Clearinghouse for Educational Facilities recommends that schools retain the services of a landscape architect. The American Society of Landscape Architects (ALSA) in Washington, D.C. can assist the teacher leader or parent in locating a qualified professional through the local ASLA Chapter closest to the school site.

Every child should have the opportunity to use his or her imagination, play vigorously, and socialize with friends within an environment that includes grass, trees, and natural scenery. A trip to the local nursery is a great start.

**Figure One**

Vigorous Physical Play Movements

Advancing, Charging, Climbing, Crawling, Darting, Dashing, Dodging, Fluttering, Flying, Galloping, Jumping, Leaping, Marching, Roaming, Rolling, Running, Scampering, Scattering, Searching, Shuffling, Skating, Skipping, Sliding, Slithering, Sneaking, Strolling, Strutting, Surrounding, Tiptoeing, Tramping, Trudging, Waddling, Walking, and Wandering.

**Figure Two**

Sample Shapes the Body Can Make

Box, Long, Narrow, Twisted, Bridge Shape, Flat, Wide, Tall, Crooked, Round.

**Figure Three**

Non-Vigorous Physical Play Movements

Arching, Balancing, Bending, Bobbing, Bouncing, Bursting, Clapping, Collapsing, Crumbling, Curling, Ducking, Freezing, Grabbing, Inflating, Jerking, Kneeling, Leaning, Lifting, Pulling, Pushing, Rising, Shaking, Spinning, Stamping, Stretching, Swaying, Trembling, Tugging, Turning, Twisting, Whirling, Wiggling.

**Figure Four**

Elements of Communication

Common to Make-Believe Play

Listening

Describing

Naming

Identifying

Questioning

Explaining or Describing

Imitating or Mimicking

Creative Thinking

Cooperating

Role-Playing

Listening

Analyzing or Strategizing

Problem Solving

Symbolizing

Displaying Verbal Emotions

Risk Taking

Exploring

Discovering

Adapting

Inventing

**Figure Five**

**Typical Make-Believe Themes**

Fleeing from Monsters

Treasure Hunting

Volcano and other Disasters

Playing Hospital

Police Station

Using Lookout Towers

Make-believe Space Travel

Visiting Dinosaurland

Wizards and Magic

Cartoon Characters

Comic book Super Heroes

Storybook Characters

Villains

**Figure Six**

**Common Native Shrubs
in North America**

American arborvitae

American Beautyberry

Bayberry

Bottlebrush Buckeye

California Lilac

Carolina Allspice

Dwarf Fothergilla

Mountain Laurel

Oakleaf Hydrangea

Oregon Grapeholly

Serviceberry

Virginia Sweetspire

### *Notes*

Chen, M. (1994). *The Smart Parents Guide to Kid's TV.* San Francisco: KQED Books.

Clements, R. (2004). "An Investigation of the Status of Outdoor Play," *Contemporary Issues in Early Childhood Education.* International/Refereed/On-line Journal. Vol. 5, 1, 68-90.

Cobb, E. (1977). *The Ecology of Imagination in Childhood.* New York: Columbia University Press.

Frost, J.L., Wortham, S., & Reifel, S. (2001). *Play and Child Development.* NJ: Merrill Prentice Hall.

Grotowsky, J. (1968). *Towards a Poor Theatre.* New York: Simon and Schuster.

Hartle, L. (1996). "Effects of additional materials on preschool children's outdoor play behaviors," *Journal of Research in Childhood Education*, 11, (1), 68-81.

Kampmann, Jan, Barnet og det fysiske rum. (1994). *The Child and the Physical Space.* Copenhagen: Børn & Unge.

Moore, R. C. & Wong, H.H. (1997). *Natural Learning: Creating Environments for Rediscovering Nature's Way of Teaching.* Berkeley, Calif.: MIG Communications.

Vygotsky, L.S. (1978). *Mind in Society.* Cambridge, Mass.: Harvard University Press.

Winnicott, D.S. (1971). *Playing and Reality.* New York: Basic Books.

# Barton J. Hirsch

# AFTER-SCHOOL PROGRAMS

## Positive Places in Unsafe Urban Environments

**Barton J. Hirsch is professor of human development and social policy at Northwestern University where he is also on the faculty of the Institute for Policy Research. His recent book *Boys & Girls Clubs, A Place to Call Home: After-School Programs for Urban Youth* received the 2006 Social Policy Award for Best Authored Book from the Society for Research on Adolescence. Hirsch is Fellow of the American Psychological Association and of the Society for Community Research and Action.**

The old Cat Stevens song asks "where do the children play?". This question has always been an issue for low-income minority youth who live in large cities. Back in the 1920s, New York City built 225 new playgrounds, but only two of these were built in African American neighborhoods (Reiss, 1989). Nowadays, parks are where drug dealers hang out and large groups of young people on city streets attract the attention of gangs (Flynn, 1999).

After-school programs are one place where urban youth can spend time in a generally safe environment. After-school programs take place after the conclusion of the school day, from 3–6 p.m. weekdays. They can be found in a wide variety of settings: schools, park districts, museums, libraries, and community-based organizations. Policy makers are increasingly focused on how they can help to achieve a number of important goals, from promoting positive youth development and workforce preparation to decreasing rates of school drop-out and problem behavior. Guided activities and relationships with caring staff can lead to important developmental gains by increasing skills, instilling confidence, broadening cultural horizons, promoting positive values, and pointing youth in the right direction as they grow up (Benson, 1997; Hirsch, 2005; Lerner, 2004; Mahoney, Larson, & Eccles, 2005; National Research Council, 2002; Noam, Biancaosa, & Dechausay, 2003; Pittman, Irby, & Ferber, 2000).

After-school programs can differ dramatically in focus. Those which are academically oriented provide considerable tutoring to supplement classroom efforts. Other programs specialize in a skill domain, such as an athletic or artistic activity. For high school youth, apprenticeship oriented programs are often attractive (Halpern, in press; Hirsch & Hedges, in press). A number of well-established national organizations, such as the Boys & Girls Clubs of America and the Ys, offer comprehensive after-school programs. Comprehensive after-school centers offer activities in many areas, including recreation, academic support (typically homework assistance), psychoeducational programs, arts, computers, field trips for cultural enrichment, entrepreneurship (including fundraising), dances, movies, and so on. In the remainder of this chapter I will describe research that my students and I conduct-

ed in several urban Boys & Girls Clubs that were comprehensive after-school centers.

## Research on Urban Boys & Girls Clubs

Over a period of several years, we conducted two major studies; the first focused on 6 clubs (see Deutsch, in press; Hirsch, 2005) and in a second, later study, we returned to 3 clubs from the original set. All of the young people we studied were adolescents, and the great majority were in early adolescence (age 10-15). The samples were mostly African American (approximately 2/3), with the remainder mostly Hispanic. In the first study, approximately 80% would be classified as low-income, as referenced by receipt of free or reduced price lunch at school, whereas this figure was 93% in the second study. We employed multiple methods, including ethnography, structured interviews, and survey questionnaires.

There is a strong press in the Bush-led policy world for after-school programs to privilege tutoring and other academic support activities. These clubs do provide homework assistance, but they see their mission more broadly. They seek to promote growth in a wide range of skills and domains. They help youth deal with the many stressors of growing up in these neighborhoods and provide the knowledge, encourage the attitudes, and teach the skills and discipline needed for success in life. Their top priority is the broader educational task of preparing youngsters to grow up and take their place as productive members of society. Let us consider how an emphasis on the club as a place for play and for relationships fits this mission.

## A Place for Play

One of the first things that strikes you as you enter one of these clubs is the noise and general hubbub. For a couple of middle-aged ears like mine, taking a few aspirins beforehand is a wise precaution against headaches. Even so, I am glad to endure the occasional pounding in my head because it is clear that the kids are having such a great time.

Most youth tend to congregate in the gym or game room. The gym has a full-length basketball court and bleachers for spectators. It tends to have multiple activities going on. These activities are, for the most part, freely and spontaneously chosen by the youth themselves. They play pick-up games of basketball or dodge ball, chase each other good naturedly, engage in double-dutch jump rope, or just hang out and talk. The game room can have ping-pong and pool tables and an assortment of other games and apparatus.

Most of the staff (there are exceptions) appreciate and encourage the opportunity to have spontaneous fun. They do want club youth to learn and achieve, but having time to have fun is important too. Good relationships between youth and staff develop easily in this context.

Historically, having fun in unstructured activities has been characteristic of low-income African American youth (Lareau, 2003), but such a pursuit is increasingly difficult to enjoy in these communities given the extensive violence. The clubs provide a generally safe setting where, for a time, they can just be kids, enjoying themselves as children.

Not all time is unstructured. Almost all youth spend some time in structured programs or activities, learning new skills and developing their talents. But unlike the outdoor settings in these neighborhoods, and unlike their highly regimented schools, the clubs provide a place where they can let loose and, in their own words, be "more myself" (Hirsch, 2005, p.50).

The opportunity to play and have fun provides a context that makes youth feel welcome. They are then amenable to being drawn into more structured activities and viewing staff as potential mentors. Having fun is thus an intrinsic value as well as instrumental in facilitating broader objectives.

## A Place for Relationships

You didn't think that all of those activities were done individually, in isolation? The young people are almost always with each other, even when perusing web sites on the computer. Many of them come to the club because their friends, siblings, or cousins are there. Many make good friends during their time at the club, and the time they spend at the club is extensive: our data revealed that approximately half come all five days of the school week, and many had been coming to their club for years.

In a structured assessment we conducted of girls' friendships at the club, we found that more than half of their friends, and 74% of their closest friends, attended the same club (Loder & Hirsch, 2003). For 76% of the girls we interviewed, their best friend was a member of a girls-only group at the club of which they both were members.

Relationships young people formed at the club made it a very special place. Approximately three-fourths of them said that the club was like a "second home" and the overwhelming reason why this was so had to do with the close interpersonal ties. These ties were not only with peers, but very much so with the adult staff as well.

Most club staff members were in their 20s (mostly) or 30s and either currently lived in or had grown up in that neighborhood or a neighborhood much like it. They identified with the young people; for them, these were not "problem" or "at-risk" kids, but *their* kids. Kids with talents and ambitions who might need a boost to deal with problems in growing up, sometimes in troubling circumstances. They appreciated and encouraged spontaneity, expressiveness, and enthusiasms, fostering initiative and self-esteem. They knew and shared their culture, talking with an easy familiarity, for example, about black TV shows and music figures. And they had recognizable street smarts, able to control confrontations and keep them from getting out of hand, guaranteeing safety.

The time spent having fun together, combined with the protection, shared cultural affinity, and warmth and caring in their interactions enabled many staff to become wide-ranging mentors. Whether in informal interactions, or programs designed specifically for this purpose, staff discussed and counseled regarding all types of life issues—-from the mysteries of puberty, to what led young people to engage in violence (and the need and ways to avoid it), to how to complete college applications and think about employment issues. The comprehensive mentoring that club staff provide is one of their strongest assets.

## Conclusion

The outdoors can be a wonderful place for young people, but in poor, urban neighborhoods, they often are just not safe. And in the cold winter months, they are not very hospitable. Good after-school programs can turn indoor spaces into positive places for expressiveness, personal growth, and close relationships well worth our support.

## Literature

Benson, P. (1997). *All Kids Are Our Kids: What communities must do to raise caring and responsible children and adolescents.* San Francisco: Jossey-Bass.

Deutsch, N. (in press). *There Are Birds in the Project.* New York: New York University Press.

Flynn, C. (1999). "On Being Twelve: The worlds of early adolescents in an urban neighborhood." Unpublished dissertation, Northwestern University, Evanston, Ill.

Halpern, R. (in press). *After-School Matters in Chicago: Apprenticeship as a model for youth programming.* Youth and Society.

Hirsch, B. J. (2005). *A Place to Call Home: After-school programs for urban youth.* Washington, DC: American Psychological Association & New York: Teachers College Press.

Hirsch, B. J. & Hedges, L. V. (in press). *After School Programs for High School Students: Launching the evaluation of after school matters.* Evaluation Exchange.

Lareau, A. (2003). *Unequal Childhoods.* Berkeley, Calif.: University of California Press.

Lerner, R. M. (2004). *Liberty: Thriving and civic engagement among America's youth.* Thousand Oaks, Calif.: Sage.

Loder, T., & Hirsch, B. J. (2003). "Inner city youth development organizations: The salience of peer ties among early adolescent girls." *Applied Developmental Science, 7,* 2-12.

Mahoney, J. L., Larson, R. W., & Eccles, J. S. (2005). *Organized Activities as Contexts of Development: Extracurricular activities, after-school, and community programs.* Mahwah, N.J.: Erlbaum.

National Research Council and Institute of Medicine (NRC/IOM) Committee on Community-Level Programs for Youth. (2002). "Community programs to promote youth development" (J. Eccles & J. Gootman, Eds.). Washington, D.C.: National Academy Press.

Noam, G., Biancarosa, G., & Dechausay, N. (2003). *Afterschool Education: Approaches to an emerging field.* Cambridge, Mass: Harvard Education Press.

Pittman, K., Irby, M., & Ferber, T. (2000). *Unfinished Business: Further reflections on a decade of promoting youth development.* Philadelphia: Public/Private Ventures.

Reiss, S. (1989). *City Games.* Urbana, Ill.: University of Illinois Press.

# Mark Stranahan

## WHERE IS THIS TAKING PLACE?

Mark Stranahan is an architect and urban planner with degrees from the University of Michigan. He is an advocate for sustainable design and green development. He has served on boards of several organizations relating to children and childhood and on private foundation boards.

Children signify the past and future, desired or undesirable, savage or idyllic, sylvan or polluted. Childhood evokes a desirable future, imagined both collectively and individually by each of us.

Many adults have shared personal memories of fantasy play that took place unseen in burrows and forts and glades, in unclaimed, undiscovered, abandoned places, and in cherished children's literature.

Childhood is compressed and disordered in space and time. It is curiously uncoupled from places. There is no longer a familiar, expected geography, a distribution of places like playgrounds where the presence of children is an expected familiarity. Rather, the appearance of children may more frequently mark places in which they are unexpected.

It's easy to not see teens. If you are not looking, you might not see them or their particular physical culture. If you are looking, you will. Ours is a world of hybridity and disappearance, of the collapse of space and time in which social differentiation among us is deranged. Where there is no sensible adult geography, teens have to invent their own.

Wild, uncolonized places subsist in the alleys and on rooftops. Unwanted, forgotten, vacant, underground, uncategorized, imaginary, and empty, these are *invisible* like the site of raves. They are criminalized, categorically suspect locales of vagrancy. If a teen is *seen* here, she is vagrant and "out of place." In spaces like this, the *work* of adolescent development leaves visible artifacts of tagging and graffiti: marking, signing, naming.

## The Neutral Zone

The Neutral Zone is a teen center in Ann Arbor, Michigan. In as much as teens use it, it is successful. They inhabit it. They occupy it. They populate it. The poem by Joan Didion that appears above is painted on its wall.

The Neutral Zone is a turn-of-the-century industrial building. It has, like a velveteen rabbit, a varied past as a gritty, dependable, and underappreciated vessel for the marginal. It was forgotten and unclaimed. It was a billiard hall and a coffee house and a folk club. The Neutral Zone is a physical place where teens can disclose a succession of experimental identities.

But it is safe. It is safe because it is a physical place.

The building is an eight-minute walk from the downtown bus transit hub. It is fairly equidistant from the high schools. It is near, but not in, a transient rental neighborhood and near University buildings and playing fields. It is a block away from a convenience store. It adjoins a major downtown street, but it doesn't front on it, and its signage is cryptic. Its entrance isn't on the street but on a generous, malleable, nebulous area of varied surfaces and uncertain territorial claims where parents are fairly comfortable in their cars, and teens are at their ease.

Special places come into being because special, creative people have a vision for something different. Many not-for-profit organizations are started to serve specific people not well served—kids—and are willed into being by the charisma and sheer entrepreneurial energy of a visionary founder.

The Neutral Zone was willed into being by such an individual, engaged with such particular kids. Teens identified the problem, the need, and the remedy— a neutral zone. Teens were not only vessels of the initial vision, but were necessary agents in its beginning and building.

The Neutral Zone is a substantial place where young men and women of substance are born and celebrated. The Neutral Zone works simply and only because it is not mediated by adults. The empty space normally filled with the imagined past and envisioned future of adults is instead filled with the bodies and imaginations of teens.

It is most intensely a place of music and poetry. The rhythm and spirit that *take place* here, the guts and heart and sheer creative horsepower that riot inside, are astounding and unsuspected by many adults. The stage of the theatrical invention of personhood is conjured. It is pulled into being and held open by the embrace and affirmation of teens and complicit adults. Bodies are liberated and voices are amplified. Bodies are amplified and voices are liberated.

Finally, the Neutral Zone is a place that is so fully and ardently claimed, appropriated, written in, written on, imprinted, marked, signed, tagged, and imagined that it is impregnable, impenetrable. It cannot be endowed, or bestowed, or conferred. It is where the work of play and the play of work *take place*. It is continually imagined into being.

It may be that for most of us, the best way to make a *place* like the Neutral Zone is to go away. We are gradually outsiders in the lives of our kids and our teens until we can no longer assemble, form, and imagine them into being. When their work takes place, they are the inventors, and we are no longer magicians.

*What we play is life.*

LOUIS ARMSTRONG

# Jacoby Simmons

# THE NEUTRAL ZONE

**Jacoby Simmons is currently enrolled at Washtenaw Community College, taking classes in music production and engineering. He is a member of the Ann Arbor hip hop group Tree City, which performs in Southeast Michigan.**

Before I get started, some definitions:

Me: Jacoby Simmons, 17, senior at Stone School.

Scratch: just using the turntables as instruments. You're just making noise. It may be cool noise, but it's still pretty much a basic step using rhythm and timing.

Mix: blending two audio tracks that have the same tempo. It's a higher skill. After you know how to scratch, you start to mix.

Beat-Juggling: like mixing but live, totally unrehearsed mixing of two tracks of the same song.

I started coming to weekend events at The Neutral Zone awhile ago, but I didn't start showing up at Drop-in until I was 16. Why the gap? Well, I had heard about the weekend shows through word-of mouth. Everyone went. But even though I knew about NZ as a venue for these shows, I didn't know there was a thing called Drop-in. One day at school (at the time, I was going to Huron), I saw this flyer that said, "Get on the bus!" You could take a bus from Huron to the Neutral Zone, and I thought, hey, that's pretty cool, so a bunch of other guys and me did what the flyer said. We just got on the bus.

I was walking around with the guys I had met on the bus — Mike Hyter and Justin Nunn — exploring, talking to people, being friendly. We started hanging out. We found the studio and thought, "Wow, that's pretty legit" and that's how T5E got started.

So now I guess I had better tell you about T5E, our crew (group). It was just like a spur of the moment thing. One minute, we were just sitting on the bus, getting to know each other on the way to NZ, and Mike said, "We should start a group."

And I said, "OK, and since Neutral Zone has a studio, we should try to put out a CD."

And then we were a band.

Justin and I started going to DJ class (Turntableism) together, learning how to scratch but Justin stopped coming and started pursuing rapping more. I stayed, stuck with the Turntableism class, and got better. I started experimenting, pushing myself, doing really crazy patterns. When Nick (Ayers, NZ staff & Turntableism instructor) heard me, he encouraged me to go on, which was pretty nice of him, but I didn't real-

ly need the encouragement. I loved the sounds I was making. It just felt right.

T5E makes the kind of music you put in whenever you're bored, and just want to listen to something good, in the hopes that it will knock you out of your mood. I'd say it's abstract, different, not what you hear every day, but still quality. We put a message into the music we put out—we stress the value of individuality and choosing the route that's best for you, not just the most popular. We want to remind our listeners to make their own decisions—not to let other people decide for them. I'd tell you to check out our music and decide for yourselves, but you can't — our CDs are all sold out!

Thanks for staying with me. I know it's kind of a long story. But I hope I'm showing you just what can happen when you put together a bunch of teens like me who don't think they have anything better to do in a place like Neutral Zone, with the tools and staff to help us develop as people and as artists. I almost always have something to do when I come here. Sometimes, there isn't and we hang out, talk to our friends, scratch or shoot pool. But if I wasn't here, I'd just be hanging out at home, being a bum.

But instead, I'm a DJ. I get gigs—I've done stuff at the Michigan League, the Michigan Union, Pioneer High School, the Neutral Zone, plus a few private house parties, and I get paid for it. How cool is that? Also, the Zone's music program has brought in a lot of hip-hop artists for us to meet: Elzhi, DJ Haircut, DJ Graffiti, One Be Lo. . . . they've all dropped some serious knowledge on us about the music business from an insider's point of view. I'm pretty sure I wouldn't have been able to meet and talk to artists like that on my own.

I've wanted to be a DJ forever. I guess I was just born with a love for music, point blank. I love the emotion it brings, the emotion I feel from listening to a certain song. I have different songs in my head for when I'm feeling peaceful, or angry, songs that help me vent. If I didn't have that connection, I would be robotic—a really monotonous, boring lifeless person. But now I have other interests, other plans, too.

Last summer, I went on the Wild Michigan backpacking trip. We spent six days in the wilderness, and hiked over 30 miles, carrying everything on our backs. I didn't have any experience even camping, but the Jackson (Perry, the NZ music director at the time) and Jenni (a friend) would not stop harassing me about it, so I figured, "OK. Must be pretty good if they going on about it." The day of trip, I came in with all my gear, which wasn't much, but NZ provided what I didn't have which was good, because otherwise, I probably wouldn't have ever done it. In the beginning every little thing was hard — waking up early, sleeping on ground in a tent, cold, trying to find a comfy position with 2-3 strangers in the tent, having to deal with the smells

from clothes, sweat. . . . And the bugs were out of control.

We were a group, and we had to work together the entire time. No one else was going to get water to boil or purify. No one else would collect firewood for us. I really learned and experienced what it means to work as a team. When there was some bad blood (and there always eventually is), you just had to sit down and talk about it. It was the only way we were going to get through it. Everyone realized that the trip wouldn't be good if EVERYONE wasn't happy. You just can't have a good trip if everyone's angry at each other. I didn't know most of the other teens on the trip at the start, but now I have a different perspective on them. We have an understanding based on shared struggle and experiences that in the end were really fun. I hope to be able to go again this summer.

This year, after I graduate, I'm going to WCC for two years, then I'm going to transfer to Michigan State, majoring in Arts & Communications. I still want to DJ, but I'd also like to become an on-air radio host with my own show at a public radio station. I'll play the music I thought was important, discuss current events and politics, and have my listeners call-in, too. Everybody talks, and everybody listens.

One last thing — there aren't a lot of places like the Neutral Zone, a place where regular teens can discover and explore who they are and what they want in a safe space that's all our own.

Remote-Controlled Childhood

*When I was a kid I had a deep sense of connection to nature itself, but I couldn't have told you anything about the Amazon rainforest. Today kids can tell you anything about the Amazon, but they're unlikely to be able to tell you about the last time they went out in the woods and just watched the leaves move.*

Richard Louv
Author, *Last Child in the Woods*

*A very interesting phenomenon . . . is what's called the mean world effect, which is the idea that if you spend a lot of time watching violence on TV, you begin to believe the world is a much meaner place than it really is.*

ROWELL HUESMAN
AMOS TVERSKY COLLEGIATE PROFESSOR OF
PSYCHOLOGY AND COMMUNICATIONS STUDIES
UNIVERSITY OF MICHIGAN

*One little boy told me that he preferred playing inside because that's where all the electrical outlets are.*

RICHARD LOUV
AUTHOR, *LAST CHILD IN THE WOODS*

**Edward Miller**

# SCREEN TIME VERSUS PLAY TIME

## The Radical Transformation of Early Childhood Education

**Edward Miller is senior researcher for the Alliance for Childhood and editor of the Alliance's report, *Tech Tonic*. He is a former editor of the *Harvard Education Letter* and author or editor of ten books on education and school reform. Parts of this article appeared in slightly different form in *Principal* magazine.**

Among all the cultural and societal changes affecting childhood in recent years, perhaps the most dramatic is the displacement of open-ended unprogrammed play by young children with organized activities and electronic entertainment, which many adults enthusiastically embrace as "learning." One aspect of this change is the growing presence of computers in the early childhood classroom, in spite of serious doubts about whether young children really need or, indeed, benefit from using these machines.

One recent study of child care centers in the state of Texas, published in the Fall 2004 issue of *Early Childhood Research and Practice*, found that preschool children were using computers in more than 75 percent of the centers. "Although some authorities in the field of early education believe that computer use interferes with development," wrote authors Sharon Lynch and Laverne Warner, "the child care directors that responded to this survey did not adopt this position." Most of the children, the study found, also used computers at home.

Even educators who are skeptical about the value of computer use by young children find themselves under increasing pressure to incorporate advanced technologies in their classrooms and to spend time teaching young children "computer literacy" skills. The pressure comes from parents who are concerned that their youngsters will fall behind other children who are learning how to manipulate a mouse, send an e-mail, and even put together a PowerPoint presentation at ever younger ages.

Learning PowerPoint is a popular activity in the kindergarten classroom of Sandee Tessier in Lemon Grove, California, the *New York Times* reported. "People come in and they have tears in their eyes because they can't believe what these little kids are doing," Ms. Tessier told the *Times*.

Those teary-eyed parents are convinced that knowing how to operate a computer is the key to later success in school and in the job market. And they assume that the earlier a child starts to use high-tech tools, the better. They are the reason that software for toddlers and preschoolers is one of the fastest growing niches of the technology business.

## Earlier Is Not Better

The problem is that, according to most child development experts, the earlier-the-better assumption is dead wrong. The primary work of the young child, according to Tufts University psychologist David Elkind, is to master the skills of regulating emotions; solving problems; developing flexibility, imagination, and persistence; paying attention; coordinating body movement; and negotiating social situations. There is no evidence that young children learn these skills better through high technology, and abundant evidence that they learn them best through direct interaction with other people.

In short, as educational psychologist Jane Healy puts it, "the preschooler needs experiences in managing his own mind—not having it distracted or programmed from outside. If these foundations are neglected during a critical period, they may be difficult—or even impossible—to regain." Healy believes that starting children on computers too early is far worse than starting them too late.

"The immature human brain neither needs nor profits from attempts to 'jump start' it," says Healy. "The fact that this phrase is being successfully used to sell technology for toddlers illustrates our ignorance of early childhood development."

Many parents point out that their young

children are fascinated by computers and other electronic gadgets. (Children are, of course, naturally interested in anything that commands the rapt attention of their parents.) Moreover, they want their offspring to be precocious. And they see the computer as a powerful motivator of learning—something that they believe children must be enticed into. But as Professor Lilian Katz of the University of Illinois says, "Children do not have to be amused, cajoled, or tricked into learning. This is only an American problem and it's disrespectful of children."

## The Decline of Imaginative Play

In the study of Texas child care centers cited above, program directors said that one of the main goals of children's computer use was "promoting exploration and play." Yet there is growing evidence that computer "play" is just the opposite of the kind of imaginative, child-initiated play that has long been seen as the foundation of the early childhood curriculum.

Educators are reporting that many of the young children they see are adept at playing video games, pushing buttons, and operating a mouse, but show an alarming lack of imagination. Experienced kindergarten teachers in Atlanta who were interviewed by researchers at Georgia State University in 2004 said that children were not as able to engage in open-ended imaginative play as they used to be.

One teacher remarked, "Students have a hard time creating imaginary situations at play time. They mimic or copy TV shows that they observe as they play. . . . The loss of a free creative imagination will make it hard for students in the future to write creative stories and create original artwork." Another teacher, recently retired after a 32-year career, reported that "children today don't have an imagination. Ten years ago they would make up plays, do puppet shows, make cities out of Legos and blocks. Today you hear them talking on the phone imitating something they have heard."

Today the average U.S. child sits in front of television, video, and computer screens for four to five hours per day. As screen time increases, time spent in creative play decreases. A study by Sandra Hofferth and others showed that in 1997 six- to eight-year-olds spent only 25 minutes per day in imaginative play. Just five years later imaginative play time had dropped by more than one-third, to 16 minutes per day.

Time spent on computers is not the only factor contributing to the loss of creative play. Academic pressure also plays a role. The increased emphasis on early literacy and numeracy in kindergarten and preschool education has squeezed time for open-ended play and in some cases eliminated it entirely. One teacher in the Atlanta study said that parents were the driving force eliminating play from kindergarten.

Parents have told her, she said, that play is a "waste of time" and that they were paying for their children to "learn."

Early childhood education is thus in a process of radical transformation—in which play and other activities that promote social and emotional learning are being replaced by academic drills designed to improve early literacy and numeracy. Part of this push for more academic "rigor" in the early childhood curriculum is the requirement that schools teach "technology literacy." State and local technology education standards increasingly require teachers to integrate computers in lessons for all students, from preschool on up.

The model standards for technology literacy developed by the International Society for Technology in Education, for example, specify that, before completing second grade, children should be able to "use input devices (e.g., mouse, keyboard, remote control) and output devices (e.g., monitor, printer) to successfully operate computers, VCRs, audiotapes, and other technologies," and that, with support from adults or other students, they should be creating "multimedia products" and "gathering information" and communicating over the Internet.

Many technology literacy programs pay lip service to "developmentally appropriate" activities, but nearly all of them seem guided more by what children *can* do with computers than by a deep understanding of what young children *need* to help their intellectual and emotional lives unfold and thrive. Technology education should be guided not by a focus on tools but rather by the activities that help children develop their full capacities. This, in turn, will govern what tools they should use at different ages.

## A New Literacy of Technology

The Alliance for Childhood, a nonprofit partnership of educators, health professionals, and researchers, has published a report called *Tech Tonic: Towards a New Literacy of Technology*, which questions the wisdom of infusing early education with advanced technologies. It proposes a set of basic principles for technology education from early childhood through high school that are solidly grounded in the developmental needs of children and based on a much broader conception of technology literacy than the one behind most current standards.

Current efforts to create high-tech classrooms often aim to make the technology "invisible." *Tech Tonic*'s conception of technology literacy would do just the opposite—that is, it would bring technology, along with the thinking behind it, into full visibility so that it can be closely examined and critiqued. "Education is, at its heart, a process of unveiling the world," the authors of *Tech Tonic* write. "To give our children tools that are shrouded in a darkness the children cannot penetrate is absurd.

To transform those 'black boxes' into invisible ones merely places them further beyond the curiosity of children, beyond even the knowledge that there is something to be curious about."

For elementary school children and preschoolers, *Tech Tonic* argues, the use of any technology should be determined by its ability to support and deepen what the Alliance calls "the healthy essentials" of childhood. These include:

- Close relationships with responsible adults.

- Direct knowledge of the living world of nature, developed through outdoor play, exploration, and gardening.

- Time every day for child-initiated play.

- Music, drama, puppetry, dance, painting, and the other arts, offered both as separate classes and as a kind of yeast to bring the full range of other academic subjects to life.

- Hands-on lessons, handcrafts, and other physically engaging activities, which literally embody the most effective first lessons for young children in the sciences, mathematics, and technology.

- Rich face-to-face language experiences, including conversation, poetry, storytelling, and books read aloud.

- Time and space for children to create meaning and experience a sense of the sacred

Lowell Monke, an award-winning technology teacher who is now professor of education at Wittenberg University, argues that there is always a potential conflict between using tools, which extend human powers outward, and healthy child development, which is concerned with increasing the inner capacities of the child. A microphone, for example, both amplifies a child's voice and removes the necessity of developing her own ability to project her voice.

Monke notes that today's youth are both the most mobile in history and probably the least physically fit, thanks in part to a variety of energy-saving transportation and communication technologies. In our schools, word processors have made it possible for children to hand in long essays with no spelling errors, while they are themselves barely able to spell. As Marshall McLuhan said, all technologies both amplify and amputate.

With that caution in mind, *Tech Tonic* proposes a new definition of technology literacy: "The mature capacity to participate creatively, critically, and responsibly in making technological choices that serve democracy, ecological sustainability, and a just society." To be technologically literate requires that we judge technology's impact on our lives according to some set of values that transcend mere technical virtuosity. It requires a commitment to strive to understand how technologies serve and threaten social justice, and the ways in which technical innovations affect the prospects for life, both human and nonhuman, on this planet.

"In paying attention to these values in our schools," the authors of *Tech Tonic* write, "we establish technology within the sphere of political discourse, a matter to be studied and addressed democratically, not solely by experts immune from public oversight."

## Seven Key Reforms

In *Tech Tonic* the Alliance for Childhood calls for seven reforms to help create a new literacy of technology:

1. Make human relationships and a commitment to strong communities a top priority.

2. Color childhood green to emphasize children's relationships with the rest of the living world.

3. Foster creativity every day, with time for the arts and play.

4. Put community-based research and action at the heart of the science and technology curriculum.

5. Declare one day a week an electronic entertainment–free zone.

6. End marketing aimed at children.

7. Shift spending from unproven high-tech products in the classroom to children's unmet basic needs.

The Alliance for Childhood aims to slow down, at least a little, the rush to put computers screens in front of toddlers and preschoolers. But the larger goal of the Alliance in publishing its report is to open up a wide-ranging debate about the proper role of advanced technologies in young children's lives.

Reasonable people may differ about the details, but we can agree on this: all children deserve a healthy, active childhood that helps them grow into compassionate, thoughtful, courageous, and resourceful adults—willing and able to participate in the daunting technological choices that lie ahead.

**Parts of this article appeared in slightly different form in the September/October 2005 issue of *Principal Magazine*.**

## Literature

Alliance for Childhood, *Tech Tonic: Towards a New Literacy of Technology,* College Park, MD: Alliance for Childhood, 2004. Available online at http://www.allianceforchildhood.org.

Alliance for Childhood, "The Disappearance of Creative Play: A Pilot Study of Experienced Kindergarten Teachers in Atlanta, Georgia," July 2004; available from the Alliance for Childhood, P.O. Box 444, College Park, MD 20741.

Elkind, David, *The Hurried Child: Growing Up Too Fast Too Soon* (third edition); New York: Perseus Books, 2001.

Guernsey, Lisa, "PowerPoint Invades the Classroom," *New York Times,* May 31, 2001.

Healy, Jane M., *Failure to Connect: How Computers Affect Our Children's Minds—and What We Can Do About It;* New York: Simon & Schuster, 1998.

Hofferth, Sandra L., and J. F. Sandberg, "Changes in American Children's Use of Time, 1981-1997," in T. Owens and S. Hofferth (eds.), *Advances in Life Course Research Series: Children at the Millennium: Where Have We Come From, Where Are We Going?* New York: Elsevier Science, 2001. (Note: data quoted above are from recent unpublished findings of this ongoing research, and were supplied by Dr. Hofferth of the Family Studies Department, University of Maryland.)

International Society for Technology in Education, *National Educational Technology Standards for Students,* published in collaboration with the Milken Exchange, June 1998. Available online at http://cnets.iste.org/students/s_stands.html.

Lynch, Sharon A., and Laverne Warner, "Computer Use in Preschools: Directors' Reports of the State of the Practice," *Early Childhood Research and Practice,* Vol. 6, No. 2 (Fall 2004). Available online at http://ecrp.uiuc.edu/v6n2/lynch.html.

Monke, Lowell, and R. W. Burniske, *Breaking Down the Digital Walls: Learning to Teach in a Post-Modem World;* Albany: SUNY Press, 2001.

**Diane E. Levin**

# PROBLEM SOLVING DEFICIT DISORDER

## Programmed Play in Korea and the United States

**Diane E. Levin is a professor of education at Wheelock College in Boston, where she teaches "The Meaning and Development of Play" and a summer institute on Media Education. She has published six books and is currently writing So Sexy So Soon (co-author). She is a founder of Teachers Resisting Unhealthy Children's Entertainment (TRUCE) that prepares materials to help parents deal with the media and commercial culture in their children's lives and the Campaign for a Commercial-Free Childhood (CCFC) that educates the public about commercial exploitation of children.**

In November 2005, I participated in an early childhood educators' conference in South Korea. One of the highlights occurred on a tour of Seoul organized for foreign guests. In a parking lot, awaiting the opening of a very impressive palace, was a group of about twelve 8-year-old children on a school trip. They had gotten out of their bus and were standing by a large tree with beautifully colored autumn leaves. As I watched them, one child caught a leaf that was floating to the ground. He paused a moment, took off his jacket, and threw it up into the tree. As it fell, it brought down at least a dozen more leaves that he, and a couple of other children tried to catch. Several other children began to throw their jackets into the tree and they all tried to catch the resulting falling leaves. They began calling out. Our translator said the children were counting how many leaves they had caught. They compared their catches with one another before throwing their coats up in the air again. After several throwing and catching cycles, the activity evolved into a game in which one child loudly called out what my Korean tour leader told us was "one, two, three." Then all the children threw up their coats in unison and cheered as they ran around catching the flood of leaves that came cascading down. After about 15 minutes, their teacher called them over to go into the palace that was about to open. The activity was over.

When the children lined up to leave, I marveled at:

• how resourceful they were at creating a game using nothing but leaves and coats;

• how the game evolved and changed over time in a natural and spontaneous way;

• how quickly it became a cooperative activity involving the whole group without discussion, stress, or rules;

• how even in a cramped space, no adult limit setting or intervention was necessary; and,

• how long it had been since I had seen a spontaneous, joyful and playful creation of this sort occur among children in the United States.

The Korean children's play reminded me of something I had seen a few months before in a classroom closer to home, at a preschool in the United States. The teacher put play dough on a small table. A child sat down, poked and squeezed it a few times, and left the table. Then another child came over, poked it, and asked, "What does it do?" When I was a group therapist of emotionally disturbed young children and then as a kindergarten teacher many years ago, play dough was a favorite material for both the children and me. It offered endless possibilities that could grow, change, and evolve based in the age, stage, experience, and interests of each child.

When I describe to other teachers the bored or puzzled reactions to play dough I have observed among many children in the U.S., they often nod knowingly and say that they encounter more and more children who have trouble engaging in open-ended play. As I watched these children fail to interact with play dough, I worried that they were missing out on most of the social, emotional, and cognitive learning opportunities that the South Korean children created so spontaneously with the leaves.

## Play in Development and Learning

Comparing Korean children's play with U.S. children's lack of play concerns me because play is a primary vehicle through which children learn to interact with, control, and master their world (Levin, 1997; 2003). Creative play has enormous power in promoting children's development and learning. It is in play that children find interesting problems to work on ("How can I make the most leaves fall from the tree?") and develop the skills for solving them ("If we all work together and throw our coats up into the tree, we can get the most leaves to fall!").

When children see themselves as *problem finders* and *problem solvers*, they develop curiosity about their world and confidence in their ability to figure things out for themselves. They come to look at the world with a lens that says, "I can do it!" and "I want to do it." Solving one problem leads to a new problem, which they solve by using the skills they developed from solving previous problems. In the course of playing this way, children develop deep interests, improve at, and become "experts" at problem solving. This problem-finding and -solving process provides a powerful foundation that helps children be motivated, competent learners who are actively engaged with their environment in school and in life.

## Problem Solving Deficit Disorder

What if children do not become problem solvers and experts in tasks of their own choosing over which they have control? They often develop what I call PSDD—Problem Solving Deficit Disorder (Lohr, 2003; Meltz, 2004).

## What Is PSDD?

The concept of PSDD grew out of my work on the impact of contemporary society on children. Parents and professionals describe children who say they're bored a lot. They have trouble becoming deeply engaged in unstructured activities. They lack creativity and imagination and experience difficulty in playing cooperatively with others or resolving conflicts without aggression. They do better when they're told what to do. They prefer structured activities at school or DVDs to watch or videogames to play at home. They ask for new things all the time but quickly become bored once they have them. When they're able, parents often enroll their children in organized after-school activities so they won't be bored or spend their free time watching TV. When their children are home, they worry that they use the TV and other electronics too much as babysitters.

PSDD describes the condition in which children are no longer active agents of their involvement with the world. It interferes with their ability to engage in play that promotes optimal development, learning, social skills, and conflict resolution. In the long run, it can lead to remote controlled people who exhibit conformist behavior, accept orders without questioning, and miss out on the joy the Korean children demonstrated in their play.

## What Causes PSDD?

Several factors contribute to PSDD. These include:

•The replacement of free time and free-play activities with media such as TV, video games, computers and DVDs. It involves children in a world of someone else's choosing rather than their own (Levin, 1998; Steyer, 2002).

• Highly structured toys, including sophisticated electronic toys and toys linked to media, that tell children what and how to play and that help them imitate the scripts they see on the screen (Levin & Carlsson-Paige, 2006).

• The growing emphasis on academic, skill-based curricula in early childhood settings that undermine children's creative play and problem solving.

• An increasingly commercial culture that teaches young children "I want it" rather than "I can do it" (Levin, 2005). "I can do it" is an essential part of problem solving, playing and learning. (See: commercialfreechildhood.org).

**Finding a Cure!**

Understanding PSDD and its causes and impact on children can give us a powerful tool for meeting children's needs through play. Parents and educators can:

• Limit children's involvement with electronic media;

• Encourage creative play in which children are the scriptwriters, directors, and actors;

• Help children find problems to solve and strategies for doing so;

• Choose toys and play materials that allow children to be the creators of what happens (see www.truceteachers.org);

• Create connections between parents and early childhood professionals supporting creative play and problem solving; and,

• Become advocates for creative play.

## References and Resources

Levin, D. (September/October, 2004). From "I Want It!" to "I Can Do It!" Promoting Healthy Development in the Consumer Culture. *Child Care Information Exchange*.

Levin, D. (2003). *Teaching Young Children in Violent Times: Building a Peaceable Classroom* (2nd Edition). Cambridge, MA: Educators for Social Responsibility and Washington, DC: National Association for the Education of Young Children.

Levin, D. (1998). *Remote Control Childhood? Combating the Hazards of Media Culture*. Washington, DC: NAEYC.

Levin, D. (1996). Endangered Play, Endangered Development: A Constructivist View of the Role of Play in Development and Learning. *Playing for Keeps,* A. Phillips (Ed.). St. Paul, MN: Redleaf Press.

Levin, D. & Carlsson-Paige, N. (2006). *The War Play Dilemma: What Every Parent and Teacher Needs to Know* (2nd Edition). New York: Teachers College.

Lohr, S. (December 7, 2003). "If the Shoe Ties, They Don't Wear It." *New York Times*.

Meltz, B. (January 22, 2004). "Child Caring: There Are Benefits to Boredom." *Boston Globe*.

Steyer, J. (2002). *The Other Parent*. New York: Atria Books.

## Organizations

Campaign for a Commercial-Free Childhood (CCFC) (www.commercialfreechildhood.org) A coalition of organizations working to raise public awareness about and counteract the harm caused by the commercial culture and marketing to children.

Playing for Keeps (www.playingforkeeps.org) Organization of early childhood professionals, academics, and toy industry people working to educate the public about the importance of play

Teachers Resisting Unhealthy Children's Entertainment (TRUCE) (www.truceteachers.org) Prepares materials for parents that can be downloaded from its website on how to deal with media and commercial culture and promote creative play.

The heart of puppetry is breathing life into anything that does not breathe on its own—an eraser and a large paperclip become an old man with a crutch; a mug with reading glasses taped over its nose (I mean handle) becomes a professor; a rolled up old sock perched on one or two fingers becomes a head, the hand and the other fingers its body and arms.

ANN MESRITZ GRONVOLD
PUPPETEER AND STORYTELLER

# Susan Linn

# PSYCHOLOGICAL SPACES FOR PLAY

Susan Linn, Ed.D., is the associate director of the Media Center at Judge Baker Children's Center, instructor in Psychiatry, Harvard Medical School, and director of the Campaign for a Commercial-Free Childhood. She is the author of *Consuming Kids: The Hostile Takeover of Childhood.*

Four-year-old Sean bounced around the office, searching the toy shelves. He rejected the doll house, board games, blocks and puzzles. Finally he picked up a stuffed dog and stared at it in puzzlement. "What does it do?" he asked. "You can make him talk," I suggested. "But how?" he wondered, looking for a button or string. "Like this," I answered, picking up a stuffed cat and talking through it in a funny voice. Sean was enchanted. As a child bombarded by the incessant noise from a commercialized, electronic media culture, he never before invested an inanimate object with life. When it came to make-believe, he had no idea how to play.

The ability to play is central to our capacity to take risks, to experiment, to think critically, to act rather than react, to solve problems, to differentiate ourselves from our environment, and to make life meaningful. Play is a fundamental component of a healthy childhood and linked inextricably to creativity. Providing and preserving physical space for children to play are essential to their health and wellbeing. But psychological space is essential as well. Children are born with the capacity to imagine. But by allowing them to be bombarded with noise by the bells and whistles of commercialized technology and the things it sells, we are depriving children of the social and emotional space for generating make-believe.

## D.W. Winnicott:
## Play, Creativity, and Health

D.W. Winnicott, a brilliant British pediatrician and psychoanalyst who practiced in the mid-twentieth century, first delineated a psychological space for play. He conceptualized "transitional space" neither wholly within our inner psychic reality nor wholly in the world external to us but in the overlap of the two. "In playing," Winnicott wrote, "the child manipulates external phenomena in the service of the dream and invests chosen external phenomena with dream meaning and feeling."[1] In plainer language, we play when we actively use external objects and ideas to express our own, unique inner lives, fantasies, and feelings. Winnicott talked about play as synonymous to creativity, as a means of honest expression, as health, and as healing.

Winnicott also identified the psycho-social environment essential to enabling play. He believed that play can only occur in the context of a "facilitating" or "holding" environment provided by any nurturing relationship simultaneously secure enough to be safe and relaxed enough to provide room for spontaneity. A "holding environment" begins literally with the way a baby is held. Is the baby safe in her caretaker's arms? Does the baby have enough space to move freely? A baby who doesn't feel safe must hold still for fear of falling. A baby who is held too tightly can't explore movement.

As the baby is held securely, but not in a constricting way, she makes some kind of gesture different from random flailing. Because the gesture seems purposeful to her parents, they respond with a coo, a smile or a laugh. In that interchange are the seeds of two important developmental changes. By originating an action that evokes a separate reaction from her environment, the baby begins to establish a sense of herself as separate being. She begins to learn to differentiate herself from her parent. The knowledge that we are separate beings from our caretakers is an essential foundation for healthy growth and development. If, as babies, our early actions generate coos and hugs and smiles from the important adults in our lives, something equally momentous occurs. We experience our burgeoning self as making good things happen in the world.

An inadequate holding environment is filled with failures that compromise safety, or constantly bombards the baby with demands to react, rather than initiate action. Suppose an infant makes a gesture and gets no response. Suppose he generates a gesture and elicits anger instead of support. Suppose parents are so busy eliciting responses ("Do this!" "Smile." "Do that!") that he has no space even to try to generate an action.

In the absence of a holding environment—whether from neglect or incessant demands to respond—a child develops a reactive, or "false," self instead of a true–or creative–self that flourishes in a holding environment. Creativity, or constructive spontaneity, in contrast to the constant compliance or reactivity demanded by an "impinging" environment, is at the core of Winnicott's conception of mental health.

As babies develop, Winnicott believed that they reach a point at which they begin to separate from their mothers but have not yet internalized enough of the mother's strength and security to survive alone. To cope with the conflicting needs for separation and for attachment, babies create "transitional objects." This motley collection of blankets and bears appear as a baby begins the transition from total dependence to independence. According to Winnicott, these items "live" in the intersection of our inner and outer worlds; they are transitional in that they gradually lose their importance. For a period of time, however, these objects actually represent children's relationship to their parents. They become crucial for comfort, or for going to sleep at night. In fact they sometimes seem to be even more important than actual parents because children cannot bear to be parted from them.

These cuddlies live in the intersection of inner and outer reality and, paradoxically, belong to both. Eventually, they just lose importance in children's lives. A security blanket may end up in the back of a linen closet. A stuffed tiger might be consigned to a shelf. Something very wonderful happens as those blankets and toys become less and less important to their creators. What remains, even as children become adults, is the experience of a kind of psychological space that is simultaneously internal and external, real and not real, me and not me. Within the space once occupied by their beloved transitional object, they continue to assign personal, powerful meaning to objects from the outer world, molding and shaping those objects to give tangible shape to dreams, ideas and fantasies. It is in this space that play—creative play—takes place. According to Winnicott—and I agree with him—it is when we are playing that we express our true, creative selves.

**Consumer Culture:**
**Endangering Children's Play**

Play comes naturally to children. They play, often without knowing they are doing so, to express themselves, to explore, and to gain a sense of control over their world. But play is continually devalued and stunted by the loud voice of commerce. Play thrives in environments that provide children with safe boundaries but do not impinge on their ability to think and act spontaneously. It is nurtured with opportunities for silence. For children who are flooded continually with stimuli and commands to react, the cost is high. They have fewer opportunities to learn to initiate action or to influence the world they inhabit and less chance to exercise the essential human trait of creativity.

Given the current confluence of sophisticated electronic media technology and the glorification of free-market consumerism, it is becoming increasingly difficult to provide children with an environment that encourages creativity or original thinking. They are assaulted with the noise from advertising and the things it sells from the moment they wake up until bedtime. The time and space available for their own ideas and images, for unhurried interactions with print or pictures, shrinks with every blockbuster children's film or television program—inevitably accompanied by a flood of "tie in" toys, books, videos, and clothing. The culture in which American children live today, and which America is exporting to other countries, has all of the characteristics of Winnicott's "impinging" environment.

I was playing with a four-year-old named Mark at a day care center recently, and because the office I usually used was occupied, I took him to the Infant/Toddler classroom which happened to be empty at the time. We sat down on the floor, and Mark looked around for a toy, reaching for a little car that immediately started beeping at him. I accidentally brushed against a ball that started singing nursery rhymes. We attempted to play with a stacking toy and were rewarded by flashing lights and beeping. Just about every toy available contained a microchip, and even the vibrations of our footsteps were setting off unwanted sounds. Noise from the toys took up all of the time, space, and energy in that room. Instead of settling in, Mark became increasingly distracted and I could feel that my concentration was affected as well: tinny music, random computerized voices, chirps, beeps, and whistles. We could barely think, let alone play. Imagine what it would have been like with a room full of children each playing with a different toy emitting a distinct, but equally insistent, sound!

**Pretend Play:**
**Helping Children Grapple with the World**

The ability to play is central to our capacity to take risks, to experiment, to think critically, to solve problems, to act rather than react, to differentiate from our environment, and to make life meaningful. My particular interest is in "pretend" play, so I'm going to discuss that first. Play with puppets, dolls, stuffed animals, dress up clothes, enable children try on new roles, assume all sorts of personae, and express thoughts and feelings they may be unwilling or unable to express directly. For most of my professional life I have worked with children using puppet play to help them cope with difficult issues ranging from chronic and life-threatening illness to the birth of a new sibling.

It is through their pretend play that we can discover how children perceive their world and the people who populate it. Pretend play provides a window into children's experience and simultaneously allows them to express feelings, try out new ways of being, and wrestle with life's challenges. Play with paints, crayons and other art materials is also a good way for children to express feelings and their world view. What's different is that "pretend" play is more immediate, more dynamic, and more interactive.

The recent proliferation of computer chips that enable toys to move or make sounds, often with very little input from people, renders children passive observers rather than active participants in play. Because children are attracted to glitz and because these are the kinds of toys marketed to them on TV, children may nag their parents for play things that walk and talk independently, or toys that whiz, bang, whistle, and hoot at the press of a button.

However, because they discourage active, imaginative play, many electronic toys, especially those that do only one thing, soon become boring. Children use them a few times and then are ready for a new toy that does something else. Perhaps it's no accident that such toys bring to mind the phenomenon of "planned obsolescence: the design, production, and sale of products—like panty hose, for instance—that break or wear out almost immediately or are quickly outdated. The problem is that if profit is the primary motivation for creating and marketing, then how children play with the toy is irrelevant. All that matters is that they keep buying more toys and other products from the same company.

When provided with chip-free toys that actually require active imagination to come to life, children inevitably, and unknowingly, bring themselves and their concerns to the play they create. "She has to go night-night," says two-year-old Marley as she picks up a doll. Bedtime is not her favorite part of her day. She lovingly carries her doll over to a toy crib and hurls her in with a force surprising in such a little girl. Laughing joyously she picks her doll up and repeats the same scenario over and over. Meanwhile, another two-year-old, Sarah, struggling with toilet training, plays at changing her doll's diaper and setting her on the potty over and over again. Marley and Sarah are happy, healthy children grappling with the normal developmental tasks of childhood. Their play simultaneously communicates their immediate concerns (bedtime and toilet training), and gives them a chance to exercise control over a task or situation that may seem overwhelming. In Marley's case, she gets to express, and we get to witness, her current unhappy feelings about bedtime in a safe and acceptable manner.

But what if the doll Marley picked up was preprogrammed, as so many of them are these days, to say things like "I'm hungry" or "Want to play?" Instead of deciding deliberately or unconsciously how to use it, it is likely that Marley would be spending her time reacting to the doll's agenda rather than asserting her own. The truly creative aspect of play would be lost and its value to her diminished.

For children who are struggling with trauma, pretend play becomes even more important as they are often overwhelmed with intense and confusing feelings for which there is no outlet and of which they may not be fully aware. For instance, children coping with illness subject my puppets to endless hospitalizations and painful medical procedures.

## Branded Play:
## Depriving Children of Creative Choice

It is impossible to talk about the impact of marketing on children's imagination without talking about media. These days, board games and stuffed animals, dolls and action figures are likely to be products licensed from films, TV programs, and even video games. A stuffed dog is not just any mutt a child might use to call a new character into being, but a specific dog with a specific media-implanted personality, voice, and life history. Action figures—already controversial because they are often equipped with weapons—are not generic soldiers, or cowboys and Indians (and, after all, many kids from all kinds of backgrounds identified with the Indians), but detailed characters tied to specific films or TV series.

In and of itself, television seems to put a damper on children's imaginative play. Ready-made visual images and story lines require less work from viewers. When children play with a toy based toy on a particular television character, they play less creatively, especially right after they have watched a program.[2] And television isn't the only culprit. So much of commercial culture conspires to deprive children of the opportunity to exercise their imagination. The ongoing saga of the Harry Potter books is a good example.[3]

What was most amazing about the initial hoopla surrounding Harry Potter is that it celebrated something hopelessly old fashioned: a series of well-written books. Purveyors of culture insist that kids have no attention span, but young readers were mesmerized by 300-page books with no pictures. As advertisers market sex and cynicism to world-weary tweens, nine-to- 12-year-olds were losing themselves completely in a magical struggle of good against evil. While media executives insist that even babies need electronic bells and whistles to hold their interest, millions of children experienced the world of Harry Potter essentially in silence, the stillness broken only by the rustle of pages turning or the quiet murmur of someone reading aloud.

We can no longer take the silence of reading and the integrity of books for granted. The precious quiet around Harry Potter was irrevocably shattered by the click of e-commerce and the jingle of cash registers. Harry is now a brand. We not only have the film series, we have Harry Potter school products, toys, and food as well. As a result, fans of the books relinquish not just money but a piece of themselves to AOL Time Warner, owner of the licensing rights. The images we see on the screen are not ours. They belong to Chris Columbus of the mega-hit Home Alone, who directed the first two films and directors of the sequels, Alfonso Cuarón ,and David Yates. Six figure production budgets guarantee lots of nifty special effects, and nothing is left to the viewer's imagination.

The experience of seeing a favorite book character look wrong on the screen is as old as film itself. Children's movies have been accompanied by a products at least since the 1950s— I remember spending hours putting together a punch out Captain Hook's pirate ship. What has changed is the scale.[4] Since 2001, Warner Brothers has been spinning Harry Potter films

into products, products and more products: puzzles, video games, dolls and other toys from Mattel; computer games from Electronic Arts, construction games from Lego. Then there's candy, costumes, socks, shirts, boxer shorts, back packs, calendars, duffel bags, and rolling luggage.

With each new film release, we and our children can expect to see images of Harry, his friends, and his enemies–in magazines, on television, and, until their exclusive rights run out, in Warner Brothers Studio Stores all over the world. Before Rowling sold the licensing rights to Warner Brothers,[5] her books were a respite from a culture saturated by commercial, electronic media. Children got to exercise their own creativity as they interacted with J.K. Rowling's imaginary world. They didn't need products to enjoy the story. All they needed was themselves and a book.

Now, children reading Harry Potter for the first time will know what his world looks like before they even open a book. They will be deprived of a chance to conjure their own visions of the Hogwarts School for Wizards and its occupants. Once they see films, children will no longer assign their own cadence and movement to their favorite characters.

These lost opportunities wouldn't matter so much if other books were achieving this magnitude of popularity. But they aren't. For many kids, Harry Potter was an oasis of silence in a barrage of corporate noise. As we bombard our children with images, words, and sounds that leave nothing to be imagined, we are transforming them from creators to reactors.

I do not mean this to be a wholesale criticism of children's films—or of the Harry Potter films in particular. Watching a film can be a creative experience for children, especially if it serves as a springboard for creative play. However, a film that serves as a marketing tool—many of which dictate how kids will process the film or play about it—robs children of creative experience.

Marketing campaigns built on licensed products send a message to children that whatever they generate is not good enough. Embedded in any advertisement is the message that consumers need the product . For children, "needing" the Harry Potter toys and accessories licensed by Warner Brothers means that they can't imagine playing scenarios from the books or movies without a store bought costume, instead of a home made one; a battery operated, vibrating quidditch broom, instead of the one used to sweep the kitchen floor; or an official Harry Potter wand instead of a stick they can pick up outside.

J.K. Rowling spent her adolescence isolated from popular culture. When she was nine, her family moved near the Welsh border, close to Britain's Forest of Dean–rural, wild, and beautiful, rife with legends. In interviews, she speculates that the setting and the lack of things to do stimulated her imagination.

I wish that Rowling's insight into the source of her own creativity had enabled her to turn down the Warner Brothers millions. Harry Potter did not evolve from lifetime exposure to television, movies, and the products they sell. His roots are in the silence J.K. Rowling found in the Forest of Dean. He grew in a space she was allowed to fill with her own visions. Of course, Harry Potter is not the only literary character whose image is used to sell a plethora of products to children. In fact, the lines between publishing children's books and marketing to kids are so blurred that Scholastic, Inc., publisher of Harry Potter with a stellar reputation in children's publishing, was the focus of a national letter writing protest when the company co-sponsored the Advertising and Promoting to Kids conference in 2001.[6] Our culture is so flooded with images of media characters that even marketing executives are taking notice. Warren Kornblum, Chief Marketing Officer at Toys "R" Us, described the phenomenon in Brandweek as "a runaway train."[7]

When I play with children, I am careful to give them puppets that cannot be identified with media programs. Under these circumstances, the children are free to imbue them with any personality traits that might be relevant to their own lives. When the children bring media characters to our play, they stick rigidly to that character's television persona and try to reproduce the character's voice. This is also true of adults. Why is this surprising? When I teach workshops for teachers or therapists, each participant picks a puppet from my extensive and motley collection to practice with. Most are entities devoid of media associations, but somewhere along the line I picked up Cookie Monster. As we go around the room, the teachers or student therapists (with some embarrassment) spontaneously create all sorts of characters. Whoever has the Cookie Monster invariably gets locked into a rigid representation of that specific, predetermined character, which, however endearing it might be, discourages any creative input.

## Play and Values

Once we acknowledge the importance of play, it makes sense that toys are also of critical importance. There's some unintentional irony in the fact that so many of these objects today are labeled "educational." The best toys are inherently educational in that they serve as tools for helping children actively explore, understand, and gain mastery over the world. Even if they have multiple parts, they are simple enough to be put to many different uses, and to express different features of a child's imagination.

Because children play to understand the world, the toys we provide them serve as lessons and reflections of society's values. That's

why it's legitimate to ask questions about the impact of Barbie dolls on girls' expectations about their lives or feelings about their bodies, or about the impact of violent toys on attitudes and behavior. It's also important to question the nature of a child's experience playing with a particular toy, as well as the toy's actual form or content. Do we want our kids to be inundated with playthings that train them to react, rather than to think and act?

In 2002, the Jewish Museum in New York City mounted an extremely controversial show called "Mirroring Evil: Nazi Imagery/Recent Art." One of the most provocative pieces was Zbigniew Libera's "Lego Concentration Camp Set." At first glance, the classic, brightly colored box and the block construction beside it evoke hours of creative fun. Consistent with modern day Legos, the set is designed as a kit rather than as a free form collection of blocks. The picture on the box, carefully replicated in the construction beside it, suggests that the pieces enclosed make a particular construction: some kind of a fort or modern army encampment. Closer examination shows that in fact this kit contains the building blocks for a Nazi death camp–including skeleton figures to serve as emaciated inmates.

Reviews of the show complained that it was an outrage to depict a death camp as a plaything. Certainly the notion of children building this model for fun is horrifying. A contemporary analogy might be a toy that enabled children to play at blowing up the World Trade Center. Unthinkable? In 1996, five years before the attacks on September 11, but well after the blasts in 1993, Trendmaster marketed exactly such a toy. Called the "Independence Day Defend N.Y. City Micro Battle Play Set," it included miniature models of the World Trade Center, the Statue of Liberty, and the Empire State Building to blow up. It is no longer on the market.

Violence, acts of destruction and terrorism are routinely marketed to children in the guise of entertainment. War toys, guns, torture chambers and toys that glorify battles past and future are all grist for the lucrative toy market. And these don't include graphically violent video games. A toy designed to encourage children to build a miniature death camp would trivialize the Holocaust. But where do we draw the line? Perhaps the North Vietnamese would draw it at the GI Joe Green Beret action heroes popular during the Vietnam war. Native Americans probably draw the line at plastic celebrations of their ancestors' destruction at Fort Apache, a model recently reissued by Marx Toys, Inc.[8] I'm sure that Lego would never produce a concentration camp construction set, but where on the continuum do we place other toys that glorify genocide or cultural destruction?

Apologists for marketing violent toys and for exposing children to violent media, argue that these products tap into a pre-existing dark side of childhood and allow children to gain mastery over their violent fears and fantasies.[9] Anyone who has ever experienced the rageful cries of a baby, comforted a child after a nightmare, or confronted a preschooler who has been treated unjustly, realizes children experience a range of powerful, negative feelings and fears. It's also true that playing out angry or even violent fantasies is a good way to help children gain some insight into, and control over, life's more difficult moments. But children do not generate the explicitly violent video games, movies, and toys popular. Adults create each gory detail.

Some reviewers accused Libera of "contaminating" an excellent toy. In fact, I noticed a disclaimer from the manufacturer exhibited next to the doctored packaging. Building with Legos has been a wonderful creative experience for children for over sixty years, but the concentration camp piece reminds me of a disturbing trend in commercial children's toys away from nurturing creative play to fostering a more constricted experience. Legos, like other creative construction toys, now tend to be packaged as kits rather than as a free form collection of blocks. The brightly colored boxes, and the instructions within, provide a compelling argument for a "right" way to put the blocks together.

As I am sitting on the floor of a hospital playroom with Annie, who has just turned seven, she reaches for a box of Lincoln Logs and dumps them out on the floor. In addition to the logs themselves, the set contains one plastic roof, one doorway, three window frames, and a set of instructions detailing exactly how to build three different structures. The original Lincoln Logs sets, from the 1930s, contained only logs—novice builders just left openings for the windows and doors. Original kits did not come with pre-constructed accoutrements, so children could place the openings anywhere. Like modern versions of Legos, today's Lincoln Logs offerings come with instructions rather than a few suggestive pictures of multiple possibilities.

Keeping a rather anxious eye on the pictures, Annie tries to duplicate one of the detailed models on the page. Before she has it exactly right, she places a plastic roof on top. It doesn't fit. We have not built the structure exactly to specification. Dismissing my suggestion that we build something of our own, she tries again to get it right. In fact, it's not clear to me that we could have created a structure much different from the three models. A building set that allows for creativity should contain lots of different-sized pieces: this kit contains only enough logs in just the right numbers to build only those structures depicted in the instructions.

Tiring of the logs, Annie pulls out a plastic container of dinosaurs. These come with plastic palm trees, rocks, and even a volcano. They also come with a plastic floor plan showing exactly where every tree and rock should go. "The trees go there," she says, pointing to the palm fronds depicted on the plastic. I place a tree on an unmarked piece of land. "No," she says, moving it. "They have to go here." The volcano and even the rocks have to go on their designated spots.

She takes out a dinosaur and hands me another one. "These have to fight," she says. I begin making my dinosaur talk. "No!" she insists. "They can't talk." "Why can't they talk?" I asked, puzzled. "It's like the movie," she explains impatiently. "You know! They fight and they can't talk!"

That old standby Play-Doh, another creative toy, is also now marketed primarily in kits, many of them designed in partnership with companies interested in selling other products. Consider, for instance, a MacDonald's kit with molds to make Play-Doh French fries, Big Macs, Chicken McNuggets, milk shakes, and other foods sold at the ubiquitous fast food franchise. Even putting aside the fact that such a toy is a blatant device for marketing fattening, unhealthy foods, the fact is that the children who encountered it in my office at the day care center where I work invariably used that Play-Doh set only to make the products they were "supposed" to make. Each spent one session extruding French fries and stamping out burgers, and then lost interest.

Another toy at the Sparks Center, where I work is a memory game based on the wonderful PBS series Arthur. "Arthur's Library" involves tiny cards representing books. But the only books in Arthur's library are Arthur books. Therefore, every game we play is a sales pitch for the Arthur books, (and the videos, television program, toys and clothes associated with the character) and those alone. The game itself is fun. But the game would be just as much fun if it were played with an unbranded deck of cards, or with characters from any context.

## Deregulation and Its Impact on Children's Play

Increasingly, we are depriving children of the challenge of populating their own fantasy worlds with characters of their own creation. It is true that books, films and television programs have long been fodder for children's imaginative play. For better or worse, they've always generated toys as well. But in the United States, it has only been since 1984, when the Federal Trade Commission deregulated children's television, that licensed products have dominated the market.[10] Before deregulation, partnerships designed to use television programming to sell products were prohibited by law.

Deregulation has had a profound and worrisome effect on children's toys, and by extension, on creative play.[11] In 2002, nine of the ten best selling toys are de facto advertisements for television programs, movies, and videos.[12] The top seller, Barbie as Rapunzel, refers to a movie starring, thanks to modern media technology, Barbie herself (and Anjelica Huston).

My daughter was lucky enough to attend a wonderful preschool called The Corner Co-op. It was exactly what Winnicott would have described as a holding environment—a place designed for children to engage in the kind of creative play that enables healthy growth and development. The Corner Co-op is still in existence. It's not a fancy school. Nor is it jam packed with toys. Mostly the kids are gloriously busy with art supplies, balls, blocks and discarded finery in the dress up corner. They walk to a local park to play on swings and a jungle gym.

I found myself thinking about the Corner Co-op recently, when I came upon news that American Greetings that owns the licensing rights for the Care Bears—a children's brand and television program marketed in the 1980s, was distributing Care Bear educational materials to 25,000 preschools for free around the country. The materials are supposed to promote pro-social behavior and to teach children "to care." In fact, during "National Care Week," a Care Bear invention designed to take place during the campaign, parents and children will be given a certificate to sign insuring that they do care. It looks like American Greetings expects them to care a lot. The Care Bears marketing plan called for sales to top $203 million in 2003.[13]

American Greetings paid the marketing firm Youth Marketing International a six-figure fee to create the teaching materials. Joel Erlich, former teacher and president of Youth Marketing, was recently named Kid Marketer of the Year by Brandweek.[14] A film, DVDs and videos are part of the current campaign.

The rationale used for marketing in preschools is that kids are more likely to engage if the materials used in the curriculum are based on familiar characters. The problem with that argument is that its very premise—that preschool children are easier to engage when teachers use familiar characters to engage them—denies the natural curiosity and delight in discovery inherent in young children who are not spending hours before screens.

Recently, a reporter called me about marketing in preschools; she told me that she talked to a preschool teacher using a corporate-based curriculum on hand washing. I was taken aback. Most of the preschool children with whom I work love to wash their hands—not because they are clean freaks, but because they like to play in water and they get an extra kick out of making bubbles with soap. Getting them to wash their hands isn't a problem: sometimes they get so lost in playing with soap bubbles that it's a problem to get them to stop washing.

Yet the marketing industry is doing such a good job of convincing adults that children need licensed products in order to grow and develop that Scholastic is selling preschool teachers a "Clifford's Kit for Personal and Social Development." According to Scholastic's website, Clifford the Big Red Dog inspires "Children to become Great Big People."[15]

The kit teaches kids, among other things, to be truthful, responsible, have respect, work together and play fair.[16] These are admirable qualities that early childhood educators have been fostering in children for years, without help from Clifford, the Care Bears or any other media-based character.

## Conclusion

Creative play is essential to healthy development, yet commercial culture is depriving children of the time, space, and tools they need. All children are born with the capacity for curiosity, originality, honest self-expression, and a delight in exploration. As children get older, these qualities provide the foundation for critical thinking and rigorous academic exploration. However, they are placed in jeopardy when we allow the bottom line to dictate how and with what our children play, when children are unprotected in the marketplace, and when commercial culture encroaches on and even obliterates their fantasy lives. The loss to children and to society is incalculable. We must all work to preserve and encourage not just physical space, but psychological space for children to play.

**Portions of this essay appeared in Susan Linn, (2004) *Consuming Kids: The Hostile Takeover of Childhood.* New York: The New Press.**

### *Notes*

[1] D. W. Winnicott, *Playing and Reality,* (New York: Basic Books, 1971) p. 51.

[2] Patricia Marks Greenfield, et al., "The Program-Length Commercial," In *Children and Television: Images in a Changing Sociocultural World*, eds. Gordon Berry and Joy Keiko Asamen, (Newbury Park: Sage 1993), 53-72.

[3] Versions of the section on Harry Potter first appeared in *Commonwealth Magazine* and the *Boston Globe*: Susan Linn, "Harry, We Hardly Knew Ye," CommonWealth, Spring 2000, 92-94; Susan Linn, "J.K. Rowling and the Golden Calf," *Boston Globe*, 8 July 2000, F3.

[4] For an excellent discussion on how big business is transforming children's relationship to books, see Daniel Hade, "Storyselling: Are Publishers Changing the Way Children Read?" *Horn Book Magazine*, 78 (5) Sep/Oct 2002, 509-519.

[5] "Harry Potter and the Merchandising Gold," *Economist*; 367 (8329) 21 June 2003, 64.

[6] Kelly D. Brownell and Katherine Battle Horgen. *Food Fight*. (Chicago: Contemporary Books, 2004), p. 121.

[7] Warren Kornblum quoted in David Finnigan, "Hollywood Gets Humble," *Brandweek*, June 11, 2001. Vol 42, Issue 24, p.28.

[8] "Mars Marx Toys 'Fort Apache' Deluxe Western Playset," description available at: http://www.marxtoys.com/marxtoys/playsets1.htm, accessed 3 September 2003.

[9] See Gerard Jones, *Killing Monsters: Why Children Need Fantasy, Superheroes, and Make-Believe Violence*, (New York: Basic Books, 2002).

[10] Patricia Marks Greenfield, et al.

[11] A good discussion of deregulation and its impact on play can be found in Diane Levin, *Remote Control Childhood? Combating the Hazards of Media Culture*, (Washington D.C.: National Association for the Education of Young Children, 1998).

[12] Play Date Inc., "Play Date 2002: Best Selling Toys Overall." Available at: http://www.playdateinc.com/playdate2002/overall.asp. Accessed 5 November 2002.

[13] The Joester Loria Group, "Care Bears Case Study." Available at: http://www.joesterloriagroup.com/clients/cs_carebears.asp. Accessed 28 August 2003.

[14] Constance Hays, "Aided by Clifford and the Care Bears, Companies Go After the Toddler Market," *The New York Times*, July 11, 2003, sec. C, pg. 5.

[15] Scholastic.com, Teacher Store, "Clifford's Kit for Personal and Social Development." Available at: http://click.scholastic.com/teacherstore/catalog/product/product.jhtml?skuid=sku3932910&catid=&catType. Accessed 6 September 2003.

[16] Scholastic.com.

Bringing Back Play

What I'm hoping is that we'll move into a fourth frontier in which we reconnect to nature, but in a new way. I'm not pretending we're going to go back to the 1950s, because the fear that parents feel is real, even if some of the reasons for that fear are not so real.

So I think we will move into a fourth frontier in which we can re-imagine our cities have different kinds of architecture, a green urbanism in which we really bring nature into our lives and into our children's lives in new ways rather than thinking we can go back to the 50s.

RICHARD LOUV
AUTHOR, *LAST CHILD IN THE WOODS*

**Robert Lavelle**

# CHANGING THE WAY WE THINK ABOUT PLAY

**Robert Lavelle is the Director of Publishing and New Media at Facing History and Ourselves, an educational social justice organization with headquarters in Brookline, Massachusetts. Earlier he co-founded the documentary production and public engagement company called Roundtable, and was a vice President and Director of Publishing and New Media at Blackside.**

I work in public engagement. Let me state clearly that public engagement is not the same as public relations. In the field of public relations, the goal is to persuade people or to sell them ideas. In the field of public engagement, the goal is to help the public engage with complex issues and problems, to help them listen to one another and to implement new ideas. I'm an unlikely person to be so deeply involved in the field of public engagement; I'm not a very public person. I don't mind being in a crowd, but I'd prefer not to address the crowd. I'm more intellectual than organizational.

In the past twenty-five years, I've moved from the field of book publishing to public television to public engagement. At heart, what I've been doing is to help ideas that I believe in have a substantial impact. As an editor, the books I helped bring into the world were often serious and thoughtful (and admittedly, usually unprofitable). I deeply wanted to have an effect, but the books came and went.

After a few years, I learned of a project being developed in Boston—it was to be a major television documentary series on the history of the civil rights movement. I left publishing to enter the world of public television, working on what would become the acclaimed series, "Eyes on the Prize: America's Civil Rights Years." This got more attention than I could have imagined. The companion volume that I helped produce hit several bestseller lists. The television series won numerous awards. I stayed with that production company, called Blackside, for over thirteen years. During those years I witnessed the rise of cable television, satellite television, computer games, video games, and the Internet. With each expansion of electronic communications technology, the ideas we presented on television and in books had a harder and harder time getting recognition. With so many options, it was difficult to get viewers' attention; with so much media coming so fast, it was even harder to turn viewers into active, engaged citizens. With my colleagues, I began creating ways of bringing community members together in structured settings for deliberation, using media as a catalyst. After Henry Hampton, the founder of Blackside, died, Martha Fowlkes (another Blackside executive) and I started our own company, Roundtable, dedicated to bringing citizens together for discussion and action. Together we helped to launch the website and initial planning phase for a national outreach campaign funded by the Kellogg Foundation.

Martha and I were drawn to "Where Do the Children Play?" because it brings together several elements that illustrate the situation in which we find ourselves. We know that children's access to natural spaces and unstructured play is deeply important to the development of healthy children—physically, socially, spiritually, intellectually and emotionally. That access has been diminishing significantly in recent years. Experts may recognize the problem, but changing the public's priorities to enable solutions to emerge is a challenge. There are numerous community problems that need our attention, that call for us to change. But change demands hard work, especially when it is borne of consensus and compromise. Change is even more difficult when we rank this problem in relation to other social problems. It is far easier to sustain the status quo, to convince ourselves that expressing concern or guilt is enough, or to hold a fundraiser. It is far easier to answer a questionnaire or share our frustration with like-minded souls and feel as if we've done something that will result in long-term change. But good ideas are too rarely implemented. Rational arguments do not often result in change.

"Where Do the Children Play?" puts the issues of social isolation and withdrawal directly before us in the unformed lives of our communities' most vulnerable members— children. This project is a perfect reminder that while we may be members of innumerable "communities of interest" (meeting in chat rooms, or posting on blogs) we actually live in a physical community. When we see our children more familiar with creatures in the online game World of Warcraft than with those in the woods nearby, or when they spend more time IMing fellow gamers half-way around the country than they do playing with their friends down the street, we're seeing a clear manifestation of changes in our communities.

Before Roundtable takes on a project, we ask ourselves: Do we think this is a problem that affects a significant number of people? Is this a problem with solutions that can be implemented at the local level? Is this problem of such significant importance as to warrant competing with existing local priorities seeking attention and resources? If yes, we then set about creating tools—videos, print support, Web resources— that help inform the targeted public and provide a structured space for local coalition-building, assessment, discussion, and action.

Lack of access to play has many commonalities across the nation, but the challenges posed at the local level are usually particular to that environment. We do not assume that our project is appropriate for every community in the nation. When it comes to adopting social changes, we have found it useful to borrow from the field of public health. When public health researchers attempt to predict whether an individual is ready to change his or her behavior, they often assess the individual and assign him or her to one of four categories. Those categories are useful in describing communities' readiness for change as well. Some are not ready to think about it ("preconceptuals"); others are ready to consider the need for change, to consider recognizing the problem ("conceptuals"); some communities are further along on the continuum, have recognized the problem and are now ready to take action ("action-takers"); and some have recognized the problem, have taken action, and need support to maintain their change ("maintainers"). In a world of limited resources, we need to identify which communities are ready to take action, and enlist them in our campaign.

To determine which communities would benefit most from involvement in the "Where Do the Children Play?" Campaign—that is, ready to take action, outreach needs a two-track approach. First, listen to project advisors, foundation program officers, staff of national organizations working in the field of play as well as field producers. From there it is evident who is dealing with the issue in communities across the country. Advisors, national partners, and funders then have first-hand knowledge and provide consulting and financial resources to active groups; as such they are well aware of at least a portion of those communities addressing the issue. Second, conduct a modest attempt at data mining. By observing ballot initiatives, voting records, governors' "State of the State" addresses, and scanning local and regional press sources, it is possible to identify additional communities that are addressing the issue of "access to play."

After identifying appropriate communities, implement the project design and begin recruiting organizations within those communities to build a coalition that is willing to address the issue of increasing access to play. They might provide educational videos to make sure all participants have the same baseline knowledge, as well as print and online tools to help guide the process in an inclusive, deliberative manner. The coalitions will assess their local challenges and opportunities for change and come to agreement on a year's plan of action. The action plan is usually launched at an event for which the organization supplies an event video (excerpts from the documentary). Often Roundtable sends a producer or advisor as a guest.

Not every member of a targeted community needs to be recruited or engaged with the issue. For "Where Do the Children Play?" it would be useful to launch a national outreach campaign by targeting formal and informal leaders, influential and active citizens, and people who frame the way communities consider new ideas. In the field of children's play, these community members might include elected officers, journalists, educators, police officials, health and medical staff, child development professionals, academics from nearby universities, development executives, business leaders, park and recreation officials, and urban planners. While bringing in local experts and decision makers is important, long term success requires that stakeholder citizens—parents, grandparents, caregivers, and children—be included in meaningful ways. As local communities form a coalition to address the issue of restricted access to play, it is critical that the planning group and public participants include a variety of perspectives. Such a coalition should include those who tend to resist new community initiatives for financial reasons, those who are likely boosters, those who are disabled or have disabled children, senior citizens, and meaningful representations of ages, incomes, races and ethnicities.

We live in highly partisan times in which ideology has a tendency to become strident. This stridency is acute on a non-local basis. Ranting on a blog or at a stranger's house party where you've just watched a propaganda documentary, phoning in to a reactionary radio program, or bombarding an offending newspaper with a wave of rabid email is very easy. Individuals acting this way suffer no direct social consequences for their behavior. However, we live

162

locally, and confrontational or divisive behavior that seeks to squelch dissent is not sustainable in brick—and—mortar communities. Access to play must compete with a host of other issues. It is helpful to humanize the issues and the opposition by bringing together people who are not like-minded, including people who have divergent opinions and are looking at the issue from very different perspectives. Roundtable helps make sure that all participants understand the need for listening, civility, and for being mindful of the difference between fact and opinion. Democracy lives through deliberation and civic participation, not just voting, and a community's ability to deal with problems demands that we put partisanship aside to make progress.

We've developed a version of the framework laid out by Everett Rogers in his *Diffusion of Innovations*.[1] He notes that groups adopt change to the extent that it has the following characteristics [text in italics from Rogers' book]:

- *Relative Advantage . . . the degree to which an innovation is perceived as better than the idea it supersedes.* The degree of relative advantage may be measured in economic terms, but social prestige, convenience, and satisfaction are also important factors. It does not matter so much if an innovation has a great deal of objective advantage; the greater the perceived relative advantage of an innovation, the more rapid its rate of adoption will be.

- *Compatibility . . . the degree to which an innovation is perceived as being consistent with the existing values, past experiences, and needs of potential adopters.* An idea that is incompatible with the values and norms of a social system will not be adopted as rapidly as innovation that is compatible. The adoption of an incompatible innovation often requires the prior adoption of a new value system, which is a slow process.

- *Complexity . . . the degree to which an innovation is perceived as difficult to understand and use.* New ideas that are simpler to understand are adopted more rapidly than innovations that require the adopter to develop new skills and understanding.

- *Trialability . . . the degree to which an innovation may be experimented with on a limited basis.* New ideas that can be tried will generally be adopted more quickly than innovations that are not divisible.

- *Observability . . . the degree to which the results of an innovation are visible to others.* The easier it is for individuals to see the results of an innovation, the more likely they are to adopt it. Visibility stimulates discussion of a new idea.

With such motivational guidelines in mind, we work with video, print, and online resources to present the benefits of change.

A single project, even year long with multiple media components, rarely affects substantial change. But if a project aligns itself with existing and emerging trends at the local level, is respectful of local needs, promotes change in stages, and shows tangible benefits, a single project can measurably help further progress in the field. For example, Roundtable recently launched a national dialogue and action campaign called "The College Track: America's Sorting Machine." The project sought to highlight the importance of all children being prepared to succeed in post-secondary education, especially in the emerging economy. It also brought to light the fact that most communities continue to track students based on income, race, ethnicity, and whether or not their parents went to college (though today this process is rarely called "tracking"). The project consisted of a three-part documentary series we produced for public television and a "Community Connections" campaign to build coalitions in targeted communities and to help them address access and equity in preparing all students for success in college.

We also began a "National Awareness Initiative," which recruited formal and informal leaders in our participating communities to take video, print, and audio materials to offices of local decision-makers, luncheon meetings or roundtable breakfasts. Our goal was to highlight issues and solutions at the local level so people in positions of power help set local agendas or allocate resources. The results were remarkable. Over 150 communities launched twelve-month projects seeking to improve middle schools through the college degree pipeline. Mayors, school superintendents, state legislatures, business people, parents, students, and numerous organizations and associations came together and formed over 110 new coalitions. Each region and community identified the issues related to the project that they wanted to work on.

These issues varied at the local level from communication (New Hampshire set up a toll-free number to guide families to resources) to mentoring (communities such as Cincinnati and Seattle established new mentoring programs) to identity issues (in Alaska, Inuits who had completed college were brought back to visit middle and secondary school students to demonstrate that one can retain tribal identity after post-secondary education). Additional media programming on radio or in print supported most of the efforts, and most coalitions committed to continuing their work together.

The issues surrounding access to play for children are many, including universal access for the disabled and underserved populations, crime, education, health, safety, sidewalks and transportation, urban planning, zoning, and scheduling. Fortunately, numerous organizations and informal groups are already at work on these issues. "Where Do the Children Play?" can help galvanize and connect these organizations, volunteers, and formal and informal leaders to make progress. Such a coalition can undertake the important job of helping children from all walks of life—urban, suburban, rural, able-bodied and those with disabilities, those from well-resourced communities and those from communities working through myriad issues of poverty—to grow by playing in unstructured outdoor settings. A national project with local applications can have a significant impact. The time to launch such an initiative is now.

### Notes

[1] *Diffusion of Innovations*, by Everett M. Rogers, Fifth Edition, 2003, Free Press, New York.

a glass or a tea kettle or coffee maker, take an instant to realize that you would not live long without water. Perhaps you are very casual with water and allow it to run down the drain without even noticing it. When you greet the water, when you feel the water, when you give thanks to the water, you and your child will develop such an appreciation for water that you will take much better care of it.

Next it is time for breakfast. The food we eat comes from the Earth. It is composed of the Earth element. In the Andean Mystical Tradition, the kitchen is the most sacred room in the house, and the preparation and eating of food are extremely important spiritual activities. Don Alverto says, "When we eat, we are practicing the greatest ritual of all, for that is when we commune with the Mother."

Involve your child in the preparation of the food. Talk with her about where the milk comes from that she is pouring on her cereal. Tell her what the cereal is made of and explain where the bananas come from. Then playfully, greet each food as you and your child prepare them. Children love this. They feel so happy, saying "hello" to the milk and remembering the cow, saying "hello" to the cereal and remembering the grain, saying "hello' to the banana and realizing that it carries the Earth element with no human interference—it is pure Earth. Then, as you are eating, feel the food, just as you felt the sunlight and the water. Perhaps talking a lot will distract you and your child, so it is good to be silent even for a few minutes while you feel the food you are eating. Then give thanks.

Don Alverto says he often notices people saying a prayer before eating but then eating mechanically, talking all the while, and not even noticing the food. In the Andean Mystical Tradition, the food is greeted, felt, and thanked, and the Great Force of Life is thanked as well.

The fourth element is the air. In every moment you and your child are connected to the natural world through your breath. Our bodies cannot live without air. Before heading out into the world to school or to work, it is good to take a deep breath, to greet the air, to feel the air, and to give thanks to the air for your life. If we befriend the air, if we open the channel of communication between ourselves and the air, we will be less likely to pollute it.

In our fast-paced modern culture, we sometimes believe we must have very fast-paced, modern devices for helping us learn. This is not so. What we genuinely need is a slow pace with enough quiet and time to reflect. If we give our children the gift of connecting with the elements in the simple ways described above, we renew our own and our child's bond with the natural world. Gradually, as one engages in these simple practices, the mind relaxes, and the heart opens. A great joyfulness begins to emerge as, more and more, we notice beauty all around us in very simple things—the sun rising over a parking garage, the rain washing the sidewalk clean, the beautiful salad a friend has made for us, or the refreshing breeze that cools us on a summer's day.

Perhaps our minds fear that we are forever divorced from nature. That is not possible. Our physical bodies are nature. Even if we were sealed up in a prison chamber with no window for light and little access to food or water, we would have all four elements with us, in our bodies. The fire element is the heat inside us that keeps us warm; the water element flows in every cell of our bodies; the air element enters us every time we inhale; and the earth element is in our bones and flesh. Our bodies are a wonderful gift. As Don Alverto says, "We are Earth walking!" We are not separate from nature. So before we go to sleep at night, we can greet the elements in our bodies, feel them, and give thanks.

Why do we think it is difficult to connect children with nature? They are naturally and inevitably connected. Watch any young child sitting on the ground outdoors with no tools and no toys. He will naturally begin to connect with the Earth around him. Perhaps it is not the children who need to be taught how or where to play in nature. Perhaps the children are our teachers, and we need to learn from them. Go outside with your children, watch them, join them, and you will remember how and where to play. And then, give thanks.

Let's not wait for the day when all our work is done to, finally, play with our children. Let's begin now, in this moment; here, in this place, to live life fully with great joyfulness and pleasure. The joyfulness that we feel when we live this way is the awakening of the fifth element, which in the Andean Mystical Tradition is called the Ushai. The Ushai is a spiritual element, what we in the North might call an "etheric" element. Through mystically connecting with the elements of nature, we bring our hearts and minds into balance. This permits the Ushai to grow. We then feel a very great truth in our hearts. We are intimately connected to the natural world that lives within and around us. Anything we do to nature, we do to ourselves. There is no longer any fragmentation or separation. We are whole, and we are home. A ho.

(*This is Don Alverto's spelling of Quichua.)

### Literature

Alan Ereira. *The Elder Brothers: A Lost South American People and Their Message about the Fate of the Earth.* (New York: Alfred A. Knopf, 1992)

Alberto Tatzo and German Rodriguez. *Vision Cosmica de los Andes.* (Quito, Ecuador: E.B.I. Proyecto de Educadion Bibliogue Intercultural, 1998)

Alverto Taxo. *Friendship with the Elements: Opening the Channels of Communication,* compiled and edited by Helen Slomovits (Ann Arbor, MI: Little Light Publications, 2005)

*Problems cannot be solved at the same level of awareness that created them.*

ALBERT EINSTEIN

# Lorayne Carbon and Jan Drucker

# TREASURED ISLANDS

## The Lifelong Impact of Outdoor Play

Lorayne Carbon, MS.Ed. is Director of the Early Childhood Center and member of the Psychology Faculty at Sarah Lawrence College.

Jan Drucker, Ph.D. is Director of the Empowering Teachers program and member of the psychology faculty at Sarah Lawrence College. The Empowering Teachers Summer Institute is a program of the Child Development Institute at Sarah Lawrence College, Bronxville, New York. www.slc.edu/cdi.

As children are allowed less and less access to the time and space to play, especially at school, teachers may be hard pressed to find ways to preserve this crucial experience, or even to continue to believe it is important. One way to demonstrate the long-term importance of outdoor play and inspire classroom activities is to engage teachers in recollecting their own treasured places.

At a professional development institute,[1] teachers of preschoolers were asked to draw an informal map of comfortable places they knew as children and how they remember finding their way there. A rich range of places, representational styles, and narratives rapidly emerged. Most treasured spaces were outdoors. All were felt to be safe and evoked memories of joyful exploration and invention, sometimes alone but often with peers. The recollected places included a park, a zoo, an aqueduct, a best friend's yard, a reservoir, and a forest. Here are some examples.

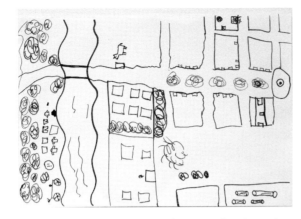

A teacher from Peru remembers navigating through "scary places" in town on a bicycle with her father. They traveled to the river to wash clothing. Once there, the ordinary chore became the opportunity for picnics, storytelling, games and exploration. The ordinary became extraordinary.

"The So-Called Pine Forest." This teacher remembers the freedom of cycling from her home through the town to get to a place where tree branches draped along the forest floor. Safely nestled within the branches, she and her friends told stories, shared secrets and kept collections of objects found en route.

A holocaust survivor who describes having difficulty recalling

This teacher recalls "escaping" to the neighborhood tree house from ages 4 to 16. The tree house was a place where the usual rules of gender roles no longer applied and where limits were challenged. An aqueduct that ran through the town "bridged neighborhoods" and the social as well as physical terrain they encompassed.

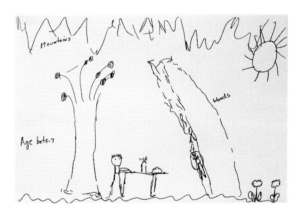

many positive experiences from childhood remembers a place in the mountains where she would picnic with her father. The heat of the sun intensified the smell of the pine trees where they sat. These and other heightened sensory perceptions have remained with her for over six decades.

After sharing their maps and memories, the teachers were sent outside to explore, each on his or her own, the area around the building and to return with something found for a collaborative collage/map, an experience they noted helped them see the familiar territory differently, through a child's eyes.

Several days later, reflecting on a week's worth of seminars, the teachers all pointed to this experience as a high point of the institute. As one wrote, "Being in touch with the child inside yourself [helps] you understand children and their values. Finding safe, beautiful places that are somewhat independent of adult supervision was key in all our memories." The memories evoked clearly demonstrated the multiple ways knowledge was being constructed as the children experienced their environments. The very lessons that even a fine teacher would have difficulty imparting were naturally learned in daily life, among them how to use landmarks to get places, when different fruits are ready to eat, and what constitutes gender-appropriate behavior.

All the teachers were inspired to adapt the experience for their classrooms. A group of teachers of elementary and middle school teachers who had a similar experience replicating important spaces with table-top blocks and exploring and sketching the interiors of the building agreed. All the teachers felt inspired to work on reconnecting their students with the physical environment in a variety of ways. Small blocks, crayons, a walk through the building and, especially, outside of it, the collecting of small natural objects, recreating spaces explored—these have become rare, even extinct, materials and experiences in many of today's classrooms. Yet it is easy to reconnect with one's own treasured spaces and begin to provide children with comparable experiences.

### Notes
[1] The Empowering Teachers Summer Institute is a program of the Child Development Institute at Sarah Lawrence College, Brownxville, New York. www.slc.edu/cdi.

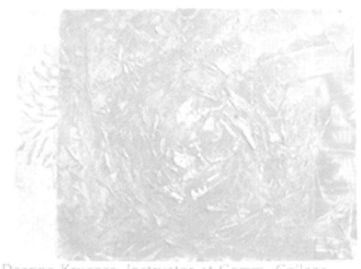

Deanna Krueger, Instructor at Comm. College
M.F.A. in Fiber

*There was a child went forth every day,*

*And the first object he looked upon and received with*

*wonder or pity or love or dread, that object he became.*

WALT WHITMAN

**Nancy Wolfe**

# THE VISUAL JOURNAL

## You and Memory Project

Nancy Wolfe, painter and educator, is an adjunct lecturer at Eastern Michigan University. She teaches the Visual Journal Workshop as a seven-day course for EMU each August in Traverse City. She also teaches a two-day Visual Journal Workshop for Wayne State University Art Therapy Department. She has been working with community organizations to help all people develop an expressive relationship with art.

The project takes about six to eight hours. Students work on it in class and outside of class.

The Visual Journal class focuses on play as essential to the process of self-expression in creating visual art. This class is structured to allow adults to take risks, experiment and have the space to play freely with ideas.

The Memory Project has become the highlight of the course for both me and my students, teachers and artists, who gather for an experience of transforming a memory to a visual work of art.

• **Initial Readings and Discussion**

We read about memory and metaphor:

"The Morris Chair," *How Things Fit Together* by Kevin Oderman

"The paving stones of Ulm," *City of God* by E.L. Doctorow (43)

*The Wild Iris*, poetry by Louise Gluck: "Song" (27)

Discuss responses to the readings and use them as a touchstone for how objects affect memory.

### •Recalling a memory

Think of an object that recalls a memory from your childhood. Is it a chair that your uncle sat in as he told stories? Is it a swing behind the house where you looked up into the sky and everything moved as you moved? Does your memory take place in a sandbox or in a hidden cupboard in the basement of your grandmother's house? Are you wrapped tight in a blanket whispering to your sister? Are you alone, behind a door? Did a shadow on the wall of your bedroom frighten you? Did you build a fort with boxes or chairs?

Students briefly write down notes about their own memory, and then they take a couple of minutes to share the memory with the class. (On rare occasions, a student may not want to share the memory. In that case, the student usually picks another memory to share.)

With this act of sharing with the class there may be laughter, or an accepting nod of pain, the affirmative shake of the head that brings us all back to moments of childhood adventure, joy or pain, a shared communication.

### •Memory Sketch

Each student should have a stack of 4 x 6 index cards or use paper. (Fold an 8 ½ to 11 paper twice to a 4 ½ x 5 ½ size and then cut the paper.) The amount of paper in the stack depends on how many students are in the class i.e. with 15 students each stack has 15 cards

Again, each student shares the memory one more time as the rest of the class sketches or does a visual response to the memory they are hearing using paper or cards from their stack. Give students an additional two to three minutes after the memory is spoken to respond. For those who feel they can't draw, I ask them to use simple shapes and stick figures and if they choose to write words on the paper, that's fine. We talk about how color can be effective in expressing emotion. Each student writes their name on the paper as well as the name of the student who is sharing the memory: i.e. To_____ from_____ . We then give each student our sketch of their memory.

If you had 15 students, each student now has 15 interpretations of their memory.

## • You and Memory Project

At this point, we now have the beginnings to expand the visual image of "You and Memory," and we have made many connections to our memory.

The student may wish to continue on expanding on the memory sketches as a more developed project: I have had a student make a separate book of her memory as expressed by herself and the other students. I have had a student work on that project for the rest of the week making different house-like structures out of mat board and at the end of the course, handing out a structure with a b/w copy of the sketch within it to each of the students.

What will the image of your memory look like now? What size will it be? What materials will you use? Will it be a 2D or 3D project? Take time to think about the memory and work through some thumbnail sketches and notes for yourself. Gather materials and begin to formulate concepts.

We come together for a discussion of plans for the project and we offer suggestions to each other. At the end of the projects, the students present their work.

*To keep one's art young one must imitate young animals. What do they do? They play.*

CONSTANTIN BRANCUSI

**Avery Cleary**

# TEN WAYS TO HELP CHILDREN LOVE NATURE

*All spiritual life begins with a sense of wonder and one of the first windows to wonder is the natural world.*

RICHARD LOUV

**These suggestions are offered by Avery Cleary, executive director of Hooked On Nature, a nonprofit organization created to inspire adults to help children develop loving relationships with the Earth, each other and all that is. Please visit www.hookedonnature.org for additional ideas and resources.**

What if we could help children find a relationship with something that inspires, balances, soothes and invigorates them? Something that is always available, no matter where they are, that is abundant and free of charge? That "something" is within our reach: a relationship with the natural world offers all this and more.

Nature is good for children and the communities they live in. Research shows that contact with nature raises students' test scores, reduces absenteeism, and improves cognitive functioning. Children's ADHD symptoms decline when their play areas are "greener."

However, in today's culture time spent in nature is considered non-essential.

Most of us take nature for granted or ignore it altogether. We are one with nature, but our actions do not reflect that reality. When

Places Families Grow

*We all want to protect our kids. We all wish that*

*there was this quilt wrapped around our children*

*to make sure that they're absolutely perfect. . . .*

*But we have to be clear that good parenting is not necessarily about giving your kids things. It's not necessarily protecting your kids from every problem. It's not about signing them up for the greatest enrichment activities. It's about listening. It's about caring. It's about loving. It's about playing. It's about reading. It's about being there.*

KENNETH GINSBURG
ASSOCIATE PROFESSOR OF PEDIATRICS
UNIVERSITY OF PENNSYLVANIA SCHOOL OF MEDICINE

*What's your best dream ever?*

**Thylias Moss**

# THE EXCEPTIONAL BOTANY OF BELIEF

## An Account that Becomes True

**Son:** The story you told me saved me. I think I'm in one world, then you take scraps and spark them up, just like how pink worlds are made in cotton candy machines. Then I can believe that clouds are sweet even though I know about storms. Your story gives me a choice about reality; that's what saves me. I make reality out of these talks.

**Mother:** *So reality is the death of dreams?*

**Son:** Dreams are waiting to be made into reality. They come so that we have something to make reality out of.

**Mother:** *What's your best dream ever?*

**Son:** The dream where I was on a train made out of clouds. My bed went out the window and became the engine. By sunrise I was back in my room with glitter in my bed.

**Mother:** *Real glitter on your sheets, pillow, and in your hair. A glittery trail from the window. I told you it came from navigation through a forest of peacock feathers. Some kind of exceptional botany.*

**Son:** Something happened on that train. Something blossomed. Pollen became glitter. I never remember anything else, as if it never happened.

**Mother:** *Is that dream lost?*

**Son:** No; it's still in me somewhere. I guess it's what makes me Ansted.

**Mother:** *Yes; it's what makes you real.*

**Son:** Reality expands and shrinks; it's breathing. It's in your lungs. It's in your heart. And reality glitters.

**Mother:** *Good night, Sparkling Dream Engineer. Good night, Shining Reality Architect.*

**Thylias Moss, author of *Tokyo Butter*, offers examples of applied Limited Fork Poetics in video and sonic poams (products of acts of making) available for free download in three iTunes music store podcasts: Limited Fork, Limited Fork Music, and Limited Fork Video Anthology. Her son Ansted is the composer of many video poam soundtracks. They have collaborated since her 1995 transcription of conversations with her preschooler.**

**Ellen Handler Spitz**

# EMPATHY, IMAGINATION, AND FREEDOM

## Children at Play on the Shore of Endless Worlds

**Ellen Handler Spitz is the Honors College Professor of Visual Art at the University of Maryland (UMBC), where she teaches interdisciplinary seminars in the humanities. She lectures internationally and is the author of five books including *Inside Picture Books* (Yale Univ. Press, 1999) and *The Brightening Glance: Imagination and Childhood* (Pantheon, 2006/ Anchor, 2007).**

Every now and then an adult grasps what a child is experiencing. You reach out and catch an invisible ball that's been tossed your way. Even if your throw-back misses, the exchange brings pleasure and strengthens a growing bond of mutual understanding between you and that child. Empathy, unjustly maligned, proves, in such instances, both foundational and generative. Yet, how *do* we come to know our children's inner worlds? What enables us, at such times, to meet them in the fullness of their imaginative play, their concentration, their joy, their desire, their quest, or in their sudden outbursts of mirth or anxiety? Whatever it is, it starts from birth. With regard to one barely month- old infant, for example, I heard a first-time father sagely say: "Max and I are getting to know one another."

Since many adults erroneously assume they cannot re-evoke the details of their early years, they turn to outside sources for help in understanding. Yet, when we try, we often *can* recall images, scenes, and incidents from the past. What about, for instance, the spoilt holiday season when your sister received a more beautiful, more elegantly accoutred doll than you did and you felt secretly overwhelmed by covetousness and envy? Or the time your beloved grandmother died and you were left all alone hurting and confused while the bereaved adults, attempting to assuage their own grief, attended to one another and ignored you? Or the Hallowe'en when you painted an oversized elaborately detailed picture of children "trick-or-treating" on a storefront window and won the contest so that your pigtail-framed face adorned the county newspaper? Still, it's hard to rely on memory and projection. Wary of changes that history has wrought between the days of our youth and the present time, chary of differences as well as similarities between our children and ourselves, we turn to experts. We pore over guides and study manuals, as if childhood were a foreign country.

Since the publication of my new book, *The Brightening Glance: Imagination and Childhood* (2006), I have had opportunities to meet and talk with many wise strangers—parents, teachers, grandparents, childcare professionals, and others—who have shared stories with me. Several of these concern the acts of catching imaginary balls. Here are two such stories.

A youthful grandmother and her husband are taking care of their toddler grandson who is spending the night in their home. Earlier that day, entertained by other relatives, the little boy has watched the classic movie version of The Wizard of Oz (1939). Trying at nightfall to put him to bed, his grandmother meets with ferocious resistance. He refuses to go to sleep. Terrified, apparently, of the wicked witch in The Wizard of Oz, he fears the witch will come to get him! He cannot close his eyes. Trying to calm him down and comfort him, both grandparents trot out all their well-honed logic, rationality, and common sense. First. they muster verbal explanations: witches do not exist, they declare authoritatively. When, however, they realize the futility of this tack, they try systematically to demonstrate to the frightened child that no witches are lurking in the immediate vacinity. Carefully, they open all the drawers of the dresser, they draw aside the curtains, peer under the bed and the rug, inside the closet and behind all the clothes, even check outside the window. These acts, however, prove fruitless. Sitting tensely upright in his bed, the little one is unmoved by their rational procedure.

At her wit's end, the grandmother suddenly senses the stoke of a lightning bolt! Abruptly, she gets it: She has caught the invisible ball. In a flash of inspiration, she disappears into the nearby bathroom. Filling up a plastic toothbrush glass with water, she brings it triumphantly to her exhausted but still anxious little grandson who, by this time, is visibly fighting sleep.

"Look!" she declares: "Here! See this glass of water? I am going to put it right down, beside your bed, on the night table. If that wicked witch dares to come in here, you can just pour it all over her!"

With that, the little boy finally relaxes. With this intervention, he feels protected, understood, and can let himself fall off to sleep.

So, we might ask: what has happened? How did this grandmother accomplish her goal? It was, I would suggest, by entering fully and richly into her grandson's imaginary world. It was by realizing that—-to *him* —-the witch was unquestionably, one hundred percent *real*. Once she accepted that premise, she could then go on to give him exactly what he needed in order to feel safe. She never explained to me quite how she got there, but I think this was because she herself did not know. Everything else had failed. And, this, after all, is how life (and art) often seem: we must fail and try and fail before getting it right.

Yet, catching the ball does not always involve content. Sometimes, it can mean just not interfering when children are deeply absorbed and want nothing more than to be allowed to continue their reveries.

Another lady told this story. Visiting recently in London's National Gallery of Art, she had sat down to rest on a bench in front of a vast Ve-

netian cityscape by Canaletto. To her surprise, a boy of about six was standing before the painting, his hands clasped behind him. He was alone as his parents had moved on casually to study other works. The little fellow stood riveted, his back to the world. He spent more time in front of the picture than any of the adult viewers who sauntered desultorily through the room. Being a total stranger, the lady said she hesitated to approach him, and, furthermore, she did not want to break his concentration. She was burning with curiosity, however, to know what it was about this picture that fascinated him so. Patiently, she watched and waited. The child's parents never interfered or tried to hurry him away. They simply let him stand there as long as he wished, allowing him to commune in his own fashion with this vision of eighteenth-century Venice and with that teeming crowd gathering helter-skelter on the piazza to celebrate a saint's day.

This, to me, is another invisible ball caught. Astonishing, wonderful, and all too rare: this respect for a child's ability to be fascinated and enchanted, this respect for his gift for timeless preoccupation. While the American lady's and and his parents' behaviour might seem at first blush like simple non-intervention or benign neglect, to the child it must have felt like a silent benediction. For, had the parents hurried him, he would have missed those precious moments with the work of art and the burgeoning of his own aesthetic sensibilities. His face, the lady reported, when he finally turned away, was rapt.

So, a ball was caught, and yet, unlike the other story, the actual content of the child's fantasy remained private, inviolate, inscrutable. What was empathically grasped was his need to look and think and be. That was sufficient. The catching here meant a ceding of control, a biting of the lip, a not-asking of questions, a letting go free.

Yet sometimes, as we all know, the otherness of children proves radically opaque. A ball simply drops. And although in *The Brightening Glance*, I emphasized the permeability of whatever membrane it is that separates us from childhood, still, all the young people we know and love and live with as well as the fading photographs of ourselves as children remind us that this membrane, although permeable, is not transparent. Aspects of children's inner lives forever resist us. They whisper of worlds we can no longer reach. Through the looking glass. Over the rainbow. Second to the right and straight on till morning. Wistfully, I recall the final image of Ernst Gombrich's (1955) provocative essay on the origins of the hobby horse: The way back to childhood is barred, he says, by an angel with a flaming sword.

### Notes

My title is derived from a line by the famous Bengali poet, Rabindranath Tagore, quoted by D. W. Winnicott (1971), in his book, *Playing and Reality*.

*Part of growing up is falling down.*

MARK RIGGS
PRESDIENT OF PLAYSCAPE DESIGNS, INC.

# Sharon Schneider and Joyce Hemphill

# PLAYFUL OUTDOOR MEMORIES AND THEIR IMPACT ON TODAY'S CHILD

**Sharon Schneider serves on the board of the American Association for the Child's Right to Play as the national chairperson for afterschool play issues. She is an adjunct child movement specialist within the Curriculum and Teaching Department at Hofstra University, Hempstead, New York.**

**Joyce Hemphill is faculty in the Department of Educational Psychology at the University of Wisconsin-Madison where she specializes in child and adolescent development, as well as learning and cognition. In addition to teaching, Dr. Hemphill is a nationally recognized presenter, serves on several state, county and local boards, and works closely with youth-based organizations.**

Research clearly proves the value of parents sharing memories of their personal childhood games and play. Early childhood personal experiences are the foundation by which we organize and interpret new incoming information. When children play a game over and over, they develop a script of what happens and when. This script is then used to organize and interpret new experiences and predict what might happen in similar situations. (Berk, 2006) The sharing of play and teaching of games not only builds the relationship between parent and child, but also contributes to the child's cognitive development and problem-solving skills. As adults, it is our responsibility to pass on personal history that includes our playful outdoor memories. Please make time in your child's schedule for daily play and imaginative adventure. A childhood memory should be more than scheduled activities,

197

movies, computers, television, video games, and school work. Children need time to be children. Share some of your favorite activities with others to assist in creating new childhood memories.

_____

**Can you find any of your childhood memories listed below?**

____ Tag Games
____ Red Light Green Light
____ Red Rover
____ Simon Says
____ Running Races
____ Running Bases
____ Tetherball
____ Hopscotch
____ Spud
____ Four Square
____ Box Ball
____ Handball
____ Tug of War
____ Monkey in the Middle
____ Jump Rope
____ Kickball
____ Punch Ball
____ Marbles
____ Jacks
____ Kite Flying

____ Hula Hoops
____ String Games
____ Frisbee
____ King of the Hill
____ Leap Frog
____ Guessing Games
____ London Bridge
____ Hide and Seek
____ Statues
____ Tops
____ Yo Yo
____ Water Balloon Play
____ Flipping Baseball Cards
____ Toy Vehicles and Building Roads
____ Riding Toys
____ Knock Hockey
____ Building Blocks
____ Card Games
____ Board Games
____ Puzzles
____ Tic-Tac-Toe
____ Connect the Dots
____ Drawing Games
____ Art Projects
____ Coloring
____ Collecting
____ Building Models
____ Bicycle Riding
____ Puppetry

____ Follow the Leader
____ Acting
____ Climbing Rocks
____ Dancing
____ Singing
____ Playing Instruments
____ Steal the Bacon
____ Double Dutch
____ Cardboard Boxes
____ Roller Skating
____ Ice Skating
____ Swimming
____ Molding Clay
____ Fishing
____ Boating
____ Climbing Trees
____ Soccer
____ Baseball
____ Softball
____ Stickball
____ Stoopball
____ Wiffleball
____ Ping Pong
____ Tennis
____ Croquet
____ Badminton
____ Basketball
____ Bowling
____ Volleyball
____ Newcomb
____ Action Figures

_____ Dolls

_____ Play House

_____ Playground

_____ Dress-Up Play

_____ Skiing

_____ Sledding

_____ Skateboarding

_____ Snowball Fights

_____ Building Forts

_____ Make-Believe

_____ Explore Woods

_____ Roll Down Hills

_____ Blowing
Dandelion Puffs

_____ Splashing in
Puddles

_____ Making Mud Pies

_____ Blowing Bubbles

_____ Building
Sandcastles

_____ Playing at the
Beach

_____ Digging a Hole

_____ Body Surfing

_____ Hunting for Bugs

_____ Digging for
Worms

_____ Scavenger Hunts

_____ Playing in Leaf
Piles

_____ Chasing Pigeons

_____ Catching Fireflies

_____ Picking Berries

_____ Other

**Create new outdoor experiences with your child or try some of these fun-filled activities.**

1. Blowing dandelion puffs

2. Making flower jewelry

3. Holding a buttercup under your chin, looking for its reflection to signify if you like butter

4. Hunting for four-leaf clovers

5. Lying on your back and staring at cloud formations

6. Using a magnifying glass to carefully inspect a small patch of grass, inch by inch

7. Catching snowflakes on your tongue

8. Rolling down a hill

9. Jumping across a small stream

10. Adopting a tree—add a daily hug, conversation, and water

11. Making markings on the ground and having others track them

12. Camping out in the backyard

13. Digging for buried treasure

14. Designing a treasure map and following the trail

15. Collecting shells at the beach

16. Reading together under a shaded tree

17. Following a salamander

18. Working on your moon tan while lying under the stars and star gazing

19. Using your hands to create shadow puppets

20. Enjoying water sprinkler play—run through while holding hands

21. Observing outdoor living creatures. Imitate their movements, behaviors, and sounds.

22. Growing a butterfly garden

23. Finding a secret hiding place for the two of you

24. Counting spots on a ladybug

25. Chasing your shadow

26. Holding a car wash for riding toys

27. Listening to the sounds

of nature

28. Watching newborn birds learn to fly or ducklings learn to swim

29. Tracking the flow of water

30. Using chewing gum for fishing bait and catching a fish (really works!)

## Notes

Berk, L. (2006). *Child Development*, (6th Edition). Boston: Allyn & Bacon

## Websites

www.ipausa.org American Association for the Child's Right to Play (IPA/USA), the United States affiliate to IPA. Promotes, preserves, and protects each child's right to play. Advocates and resource for recess, afterschool play, community playdays, special needs population, obesity, playwork, playground design, and more.

http://www.aahperd.org/aapar/ American Association for Physical Activity and Recreation (AAPAR) promotes creative and active lifestyles through physical activity, recreation, and fitness for all ages. Includes resources for outdoor adventure, aquatics, and the special needs population.

www.bubbles.org The Bubblesphere provides everything you want to know about bubbles, including games, and bubble solution recipes.

www.cloudgazing.com Cloud Gazing. This how-to guide to cloud gazing includes photos of what our imagination helps us to see.

www.gameskidsplay.net Games Kids Play. Playground games, jump rope rhymes, international games, and games from earlier times.

www.ipaworld.org International Play Association (IPA) is a parent organization with over 40 national affiliates supporting Article 31 of the UN Convention on the Rights of the Child. Play is promoted as a fundamental human right.

www.playgroundsafety.org National Association for Playground Safety (NPPS) is a public resource for the latest information on playground safety. Provides on-line training.

www.nwf.org/natureactivities National Wildlife Foundation. Outdoor activities, classroom ideas, and nature magazines for ages one and up.

## Books

Wellhousen, K. (2002). *Outdoor Play, Every Day: Innovative Play Concepts for Early Childhood*. Canada: Delmar.

# Cindy Dell Clark

# WHAT HALLOWEEN MASKS

**Cindy Dell Clark is a child ethnographer who studies cultural experience from children's perspectives, unfolding new layers of cultural process and meaning that would otherwise be missed. Her work ranges from child holidays and ritual in *Flights of Fancy, Leaps of Faith: Children's Myths in Contemporary America* to children coping with chronic illness (*In Sickness and In Play)*. Clark is associate professor of Human Development and Family Studies at Pennsylvania State University.**

As I learned from research near Philadelphia from 1999 to 2001, October 31st is a curious anomaly. Halloween inverts prevailing norms in a festival that empowers kids but gratifies adults through its dark symbols.[1] Halloween turns child-rearing conventions upside down. American children's worlds are controlled, as if hot-housed, clean-roomed or lab-cultured. Adults organize activities with developmental outcomes and tight schedules in mind. Time and space for the free expanse of play is under threat. Schools without playgrounds reflect a trend against recess, cut back for pedantic instruction.[2]

Amid these trends, Halloween is starkly incongruous. On October's last day prohibitions from sugar to stranger visiting are repealed. Adult restrictiveness gives way to children's topsy-turvy access to power threatening grown-ups with the ritual "trick or treat." Parents help assemble child-chosen costumes, bringing about an elder-lampooning parade. They festoon homes (normally a refuge of safety for children) with creepy icons of death alongside natural symbols of demise. Harvest hay bales, scarecrows and pumpkins share the scene with skeletons, gravestones, coffins, ghosts, mummies, vampires and ghouls. The very motifs kept from children the rest of the year (blood, bones, and vermin) are brought out in caricatured versions for haunted houses and front yard décor. On Halloween bad is good, small is mighty, scariness is front and center.

Kids venture outdoors even in autumn chill and hold sway in their neighborhoods. Halloween derives from the Celtic New Year's festival, Samhein, or *La Samon*, the Feast of the Sun, that historically marked harvest at the end of October, believed to be a time for souls who died that year to roam free.[3] As days grow short, weather becomes less hospitable, and the landscape more bleak. The life-ebbing season invites contemplation of physical demise. One boy termed defoliated trees "skeleton trees." Halloween is twenty-four hours before All Souls Day when children attend a Christian parish school costumed like deceased saints.

Dads and moms enjoy Halloween, as one parent said, because "children get to be big for a day." While some adults retain protectiveness following children and insisting on safety inspection of the candy, parents also acknowledge

that children gain ascendancy and agency. Children feel "in charge," as they freely trespass on flower beds or walk right up to strangers' doors. Dressed in powerful roles, they enjoy acting as and fantasizing about being superhero, *femme fatale*, fireman, or evildoer.[4] Costumed as mature, children can count on commanding attention from an adult audience in school parades or when trick or treating. Halloween is also a chance to collect booty (candy) and to range widely around town doing so.

But there is a catch for the six to seven-year-old age group I interviewed. Troubling and frightful were the dramatic enactments by adults, organized in the "Halloween spirit." Some scary displays, such as the life-size cemetery staged in one family's front yard, included a seated ghoul trip-wired to make sounds as a child passed. Ghosts in the trees and an eerily attired adult at the door warned of dire consequences of passing through graves. Even the girl who lived in this house had trepidations about her front yard display. On other occasions, adults in masks meant to frighten would jump out at children as they trick or treated. At times the bowl containing treats was rigged to reveal a severed hand, or was shaped like a small coffin with opening lid. Children gain ascendance at Halloween, yet at the same time adults retain an upper hand, using underhanded ways of frightening children.

The most sophisticated enactments, of course, were commercial, or staged for pay by nonprofit groups. The haunted house was associated with much anxiety by children, who visited or simply saw a drawing of such a place:

There was this guy sitting in a chair. . . . It was a guy who got his eyes covered . . . he was like a ghost or something, and he always . . . talked funny. . . . And then he had skeleton hands, so it looked like real hands, like real skeleton hands. And then he talked and stuff. And it was like whoa! (It) gave me and my friend Andy a heart attack. (Boy, 7)

The haunted house is scarier (than a scarecrow) because things jump out at you when you go through. . . . I think I went through a haunted house at a campground. It's scary and things jump out at you when you step, and sometimes the steps are really old. . . . It was not fun because I was little. . . . It's freaky. . . . You think the step's going to break. (Girl, 7)

Haunted houses would be scarier than death. . . . When we went in there (it) was like scary stuff, and then we went and I saw like . . . yucky blood, and there was a guy from the Texas Chainsaw Massacre, but he came out before I went to him. I ran past. . . . (Interviewer: Your mom said that you were yelling at her to go faster.) We wanted her to go fast because we didn't want . . . . we didn't want to get scared. (Boy, 7)

(Interviewer: What is a haunted house?) It has lots of spooky stuff in it. . . . ghost, bats, vampire, a bookshelf that can turn around and then

you're in something else. . . . Witches (would be) hurting people. They're mean. (Interviewer: Would you go trick or treating there?) Uh oh.

The house setting is of course the domestic residence where children are assumed to have safe refuge, a place where imagined dangers are kept at bay by lock and key. Yet at Halloween adults see fit to dramatize threats, posing as occupants of a home gone amiss, where walls move and steps give way and blood flows. At one haunted house staged in a Catholic high school, a priest acted as a murderer. On a haunted hayride a girl of about seven cowered with apprehension, crying and hiding as best she could from the adults enacting mayhem and pretending to accost riders.[5] Children also reported that they were genuinely frightened of the deathly decorations that adorned houses in the neighborhood.

Although adults may feel that Halloween is a playful mockery or cartoon of gruesome, life-negating themes, children under eight may experience these scenes with apprehension. When fathers escort their children in the dark to the homes of strangers to collect candy deemed unsafe until inspected, and teachers assign children to draw pictures of ghosts and vampires, how else would we expect the young to react?

Generally, Americans compartmentalize and distance death from everyday living.[6] At times, however, world events cut through denial. In 2001, when I was conducting fieldwork in Philadelphia, terrorists attacked the World Trade

Center in the month prior to Halloween. Adults nearby hesitated to celebrate as usual, a reluctance heightened by news of possible anthrax threats. Visits to haunted displays declined that year. Trick or treating went on, although some towns proposed a moratorium, and many communities organized alternative events. There seemed to be less pay-off for adults to burlesque themes of killing and death, although children still enjoyed trick or treating and dressing up. Halloween held comparable significance for children, but in a time of traumatic anxiety for adults, a gentler and pared down celebration was enacted for adults' sake whether or not kids were the stated excuse. The shift in 2001 implies that adults engage Halloween not just on behalf of their children, but also out of personal need. Caricaturing death and evil and distancing those themes through mockery no longer worked for terror-sensitive grown-ups in 2001. Nor did scaring the young bring its usual enjoyment when death was palpable.

What Halloween masks is this: through festively representing dark themes, adults make a farce of fear, burlesquing topics of anxiety to children. By associating these themes with children who are assumed to be innocent, adults render fears innocent by association. As Diane Hoffman has observed, American childhood ideology is basically self-deceptive.[7] Parenting seldom is a reflexive act by which mothers and fathers internally examine what they do, or compare their own understandings to how children interpret events.

As adults make decisions about free play, two issues seem hard to avoid. First, children will assert their own agency and press against adult control, an impulse made visible at Halloween. Second, there are times at Halloween and year round, when adults tell themselves they are acting for the sake of children, even as children's feelings are disguised or disregarded. Children's subjective worlds need to be taken seriously, perhaps especially on days of thrill. Haunted houses can be exited early or not entered at all, if a child is overwhelmed. The extremes of barring the door to protect children 364 days a year, and opening a Pandora's box of death on one October day, may camouflage moderate, humane alternatives:

Discuss actual human dramas of life and death that arise daily. Learning about death can be a year round project. Explore your child's perceptions and feelings when a relative or pet dies. Good books help, such as Fred Roger's *When a Pet Dies*. On a woodland hike, the body of a dead bird or mammal may start a conversation about mortal passing. These are nature's rhythms, and how this creature was affected can open an intimate talk. Consider visiting a cemetery with your child on the bright days of spring. Putting flowers or flags on a grave can help children learn about the important relationship between the living and the dead in an appreciative rather than spooky context. Along the way, adults would do well to recognize children as whole persons with perspectives of their own, no matter how romanticized they are posed in costumes.

### Notes

[1] Clark, Cindy Dell. "Tricks of Festival: Children, Enculturation and American Halloween." *ETHOS* 33, no. 2 (2005): 180-205.

[2] These trends have been well documented, such as in Clements, Rhonda. "An Investigation of the Status of Outdoor Play." *Contemporary Issues in Early Childhood* 5, no. 1 (2004): 68-77; Parke, R.D. "Neighborhoods of Southern California Children and Families." *Future Child* 9, no. 2 (1999): 58-63; Jarrett, Olga, Darlene Maxwell, Carrie Dickerson, Pamela Hoge, Gwen Davies, and Amy Yetley. "Impact of Recess on Classroom Behavior: Group Effects and Individual Differences." *The Journal of Educational Research* 92 (1998).

[3] Santino, Jack. "Night of the Wandering Souls." *Natural History* 92 (1983a): 42-51.

[4] Clark, Cindy Dell. "Role-Play on Parade: Child, Costume and Ceremonial Exchange at Halloween." *Play and Culture* 7 (2007): 289-305.

[5] Intriguingly, child masquerade in other societies, such as in certain African contexts, can also involve adults' as-if fearful taunting of the young masqueraders. See Cameron, Elisabeth, and Manuel Joran. "Playing with the Future: Children and Ritual in North-Western Province, Zambia." In *Playful Performers: African Children's Masquerade*, edited by Simon Ottenberg and David Binkley. New Brunswick N.J.: Transaction Publishers, 2006.

[6] Kleinman, Arthur. "Do Not Go Gentle." *The New Republic* 202, no. 6 (1990): 28-29.

[7] Hoffman, Dianne M. "Childhood Ideology in the United States: A Comparative Cultural View." *International Review of Education* 49, no. 1-2 (2003): 191-211.

# FAMILY REUNION 2007

## Searching for Bison in Utah

*We cannot make the past better. Ours is not to improve upon history but to document it as accurately and as is technically possible.*

STEPHEN A. SHEPHERD
*SHEPHERD'S COMPLEAT EARLY NINETEENTH CENTURY WOODWORKER*

**Jonathan Fairbanks, a grandfather and painter, is vice president of research at *Artfact*, an international online arts and antiques information source. He is also an emeritus curator for the Museum of Fine Arts, Boston.**

We had come to Utah to visit family and attend reunions. The Fairbanks family in the West gathered at "This is the Place Heritage Park," a reconstructed pioneer village at the mouth of Emigration Canyon in Salt Lake City. My great grandfather's little adobe home of 1852 was moved there from Payson, Utah, which made this a fitting place for all of us to gather. Here costumed historic interpreters explain early Utah settlement and culture. The ranger at the causeway station of Antelope Island State Park in the Great Salt Lake stated that no sightings of large mammals had been reported last Monday, July 30.

Despite such discouraging news, I paid the fee to drive onto the island with my daughter and granddaughter. They had never seen bison in the wild. But in the 1940s my father and I drove slowly through a large herd of bison in

North Dakota. For me, that was a thrilling discovery, the likes of which I hoped to share.

On Antelope Island the long road on the south shore of the Island headed towards the Garr Ranch. That route seemed promising. After driving several miles, we did spot a cluster of bison in the distance grazing at the margin of the Island where fresh water springs seep out from underground and spill into the brilliant white border of salt at the Lake's edge. Beyond that white salt flat stretches the bright blue of the Great Salt Lake. Last Monday, it reflected a cobalt blue sky. Distant mountains of the Wasatch Range and the opalescent colors of the late afternoon cumulous clouds shimmered in the hot water. The color was unbelievable. It was surreal. But the bison clusters were so distant that they appeared merely as specks in the vast landscape. We made it to the ranch and then turned around to drive back as afternoon shadows stretched their long fingers across the Island's mountains.

Less than halfway back we were greeted with a large herd of bison. The herd was moving upland for evening shelter or pasture. They were already at roadside, rolling in the dust. Bulls were bellowing, snorting and grunting while cows nursed their calves. It was clear that the intention of the bison was to cross the road. A few intrepid cows were already on the road and we stopped as they passed. One old bull nudged his cow and her calf away from our car. He repeatedly stuck out a blue tongue that curled upward. From his twelve inch tongue spurted a stream of water like that of a child's water pistol. That behavior of the bull bison was incomprehensible. We photographed the bison as they rumbled around our car. After they passed we dove further north. Again, at the springs on the shore, we found a cluster of Antelope. That completed our afternoon on Antelope Island and brought our brief visit to Utah to a close.

**Parts of this essay originally appeared as a newsletter from *Artfact* magazine.**

The world is round so let it spin.

Grant Wilborn

Third Grade, Ann Arbor, Michigan

Grass, soft grass,
  So Soft and nice, So
    green or tan, the grass.

¤ Aidan

Two Birds

they had no nest

on a hill

Aidan

Celtic Cross

It was freaky seeing a gravestone
with a Celtic cross on it because
I am Irish. It didn't say whose
grave it was, but I think it
was for a McMahon.
CREEPY!

¤ Katie

The Graveyard

When I came in, all the graves were put together,
but these graves were separate.
I wonder why?
It made me wonder about it, it made me feel scared,
and it made me wonder who they were.

¤ Susie

Getting Comfortable

At first I must admit it was very odd being around
a pool of dead men, boys and girls, but I got over it.
I stood on the sidewalk and looked for a mausoleum,
but all I saw were tombstones.

◌ Shawn

Jump

It was scary at first seeing

my name, Sarah, and Mary,

my big sister's name, on the

headstones. But it didn't say

Taylor. If their last name were

Taylor, I would   jump.

¤ Sara

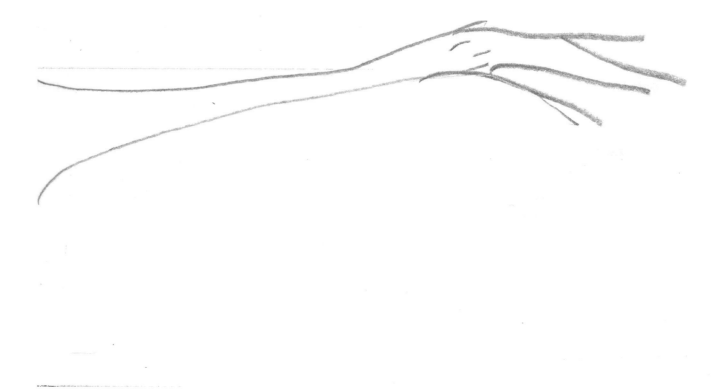

I saw
a lot of trees
I felt a part of nature.

¤ Shawn

## The Stick

Roll it like clay,
Rub it and dirt comes off,
Yellow, half-brown, dry on top
Tapping it like a drum,
Smiling at it,
Laughing at it.
Thinking about it,
Liking it, observing it,
This home for bugs,
This home for music,                    sound,
                              rhythm Sitting like a
                    tree
                    On Sara's desk.
                    Like the Torch on the
                    Statue of Liberty,
                    Like a cat's tail,
                    Or the arm of a bear,
                    Its bark was burned to ash.
                    Cracked, shiny, jet black,
                    A giant pencil tip.
                    Paul Bunyan might use it
                    To write with.

¤ Joshua, *Illustrator*
¤ Class Poem

I spy

a beautiful bird singing

with lovely notes

¤ Susie

The birds
are looking for food in the
green grass of wonder

¤ Susie

I slept as never before, a

stone on the riverbed,

nothing between me

and the white fire of the stars

but my thoughts. . . .

From *Sleeping in the Forest* by Mary Oliver

¤ Ellery

. . . . and they floated light

as moths

among the branches of the

perfect trees.

From *Sleeping in the Forest* by Mary Oliver

¤ Katie

Dedicated to Rosemarie Hester

¤ Jaclyn Cohen

# Inspiring

By Robert Kaercher, third grade

There was a teacher that inspired me
with thoughts, emotions, and wonders.

That teacher gave me all the equipment
to go on the safari of the mind.

I hunted down the biggest words
and brought them to their knees.

The descriptions puzzled me,
but she lead me through them.

The mind is very challenging at a young age,
but that's what she is there for,
to love and care for all of us.

Experts and Filmmakers

If I were to begin to describe the origins of play as we see it in humans, I'd take a three-month-old baby that's just beginning

to show a radiant social smile. Bring in a parent or mother, someone that the infant is really comfortable with and the infant

will, upon seeing the face of that caregiver, break into a radiant smile at the moment of eye contact. Both then erupt into

a kind of joyful interaction and that joyful interaction, which is obviously pleasurable for the mother and seems to be very

pleasurable for the baby, is a sort of ground base

of human play.

STUART BROWN

FOUNDER AND PRESIDENT

THE NATIONAL INSTITUTE

FOR PLAY

## Experts quoted from film transcripts

**Joan Almon** co-founded the Alliance for Childhood in 1999 as a partnership of educators, health professionals and others concerned about the decline in children's health and well-being and the growing stress in children's lives. She serves as director of the US Alliance. Prior to taking up this work, Joan was a Waldorf kindergarten teacher and educator of teachers in the US and abroad.

**Stuart Brown**, physician-psychiatrist by training and practice, has more recently engaged in independent scholarship, education film production, and popular writing. He is the founder/president of the National Institute for Play, whose mission is to bring the unrealized knowledge, practices and benefits of play into public life. Brown was the instigator and executive producer of the three-part PBS series, "The Promise of Play."

**Robin Means Coleman** is associate professor of communication studies and AfroAmerican and African studies at the University of Michigan. She is the author of *African-American Viewers and the Black Situation Comedy: Situating Racial Humor* (2000), and edited *Say It Loud! African American Audiences, Media, and Identity* (2002). She teaches, researches, and publishes in the areas of African Americans and the media (texts, contexts, industry, and audiences); Black popular culture; and African American identity formation/performance.

**Kenneth Ginsburg** is a nationally recognized pediatrician specializing in adolescent medicine at The Children's Hospital of Philadelphia and an associate professor of pediatrics at the University of Pennsylvania School of Medicine. He also serves as director of health services at Covenant House of Philadelphia, a shelter for homeless and disenfranchised youth. In the past seven years, Dr. Ginsburg has been named one of Philadelphia magazine's "Top Docs" five times.

**Rowell Huesman** is professor of psychology at the University of Michigan. He heads the SafeMichigan Children's Initiative, a violence prevention program sponsored by the university in collaboration with the Juvenile Division of the Washtenaw County Probate Court, the Family Independence Agency, and the Ann Arbor public schools.

**Richard Louv** is the author of seven books, including, most recently, *Last Child in the Woods: Saving Our Children From Nature-Deficit Disorder* (Algonquin). He has written for The New York Times, The Washington Post, The Christian Science Monitor and other newspapers and magazines. In addition to his writing, Louv is chairman of The Children & Nature Network, a nonprofit organization helping build a movement to reconnect children and nature. He is a member of the Citistates Group, an association of urban observers, and serves on the member of the board of directors of ecoAmerica.

## Film Production

**Matthew Zacharias, Editor/Producer**, has been a filmmaker and editor for 13 years. His work has won three regional EMMYs for PBS projects. Zacharias' films have been featured at national film festivals such as Slamdance, South by Southwest and ResFest. His multimedia projects are exhibited in leading contemporary art galleries. Zacharias is now at work on a feature-length film, which he is producing, directing, writing and editing. His other credit include Bus Tripping (1998); Smart TV (PBS; 1999-2000); Mahler's Beethoven (PBS; 2001); Contemporary Ceramics (Cranbrook Academy of Art; 2003); Sphinx (2003;PBS); Governor's Arts Awards (PBS; 2003), and Michigan Football Memories (2004). Zacharias' short films include Kim (AWOL; 1990), Max (AWOL; 1997), AWOL After School Special (AWOL; 1998), Ace's High (AWOL; 2002), and Good, Brother (AWOL; 2002), which were selected for the South by Southwest and Slamdance Film Festivals, respectively. Zacharias works on AVID and Final Cut Pro. systems. He is a graduate of Film Studies department at the University of Michigan.

**Barbara Lucas, Associate Producer**, has worked on institutional video projects and Michigan public television documentaries such as the "Ticket To Ride" and "Emerald Ash Borer: Path of Death" for the Michigan PBS series "Michigan at Risk," and "The Great Experiment: MSU, The Pioneer Land Grant University." She has worked in the production of a weekly public radio show, "Issues of the Environment" for WEMU-FM, and has contributed a column on environmental issues to the Ann Arbor News. Lucas is a native of Michigan and earned an undergraduate degree from the University of Michigan in anthropology. She holds a double masters degree from Western Michigan University in blind rehabilitation and occupational therapy, and another masters from U-M in environmental policy.

**Mark Berg, Director of Photography**, is a highly experienced camera operator who has worked on news and long-form programs for twelve years, including stints at four television stations in the Midwest. Berg's work has appeared on ABC News, NBC News, 20/20, World News Tonight, Good Morning America, Dateline, Today Show, Nightly News, CNN, A&E, Fox Sports, and other broadcast and cable outlets. He also shoots for the National Hockey League, Ford Motor Co., and others. He has been nominated for EMMY awards four times and has won top honors from the Michigan Association of Broadcasters in 1987 and 1990. Berg is the president and co-owner of Great Lakes Television Productions in South Lyon, Michigan, where he makes his home. He can be reached at (248) 486-3040.

**Gordy Marcotte, Sound Technician,** earned his B.A. in communications from Western Michigan University in 1988. He began his career with Filmcraft Video, a producer of corporate and network video, and also worked for ENG Detroit before striking out on his own in 1995. As a freelance sound technician, he has worked on news stories for each of the major broadcast television networks, including stories for NBC's Dateline, ABC's 20/20, and CBS's 60 Minutes. His other clients have included Fox, PBS, CNN, NBA Entertainment, NHL Productions, GM; Ford, Chrysler, and Volkswagen. Marcotte lives and works in the Detroit area and can be reached at (248) 672-3137. He can be contacted via email at marcotte@wwnet.com.

Elizabeth Goodenough, Ph.D., has taught English and American Literature since 1976 at Harvard University, Claremont McKenna College and the University of Michigan. A scholar and activist in the emerging field of children's studies, she has published numerous articles on children's literature and culture, co-edited with Mark Heberle and Naomi Sokoloff *Infant Tongues: The Voice of the Child in Literature* (Wayne State University Press 1994), co-edited with Mitzi Myers a special issue of *The Lion & the Unicorn* on "Children's Literature and Violence" (John Hopkins University Press 2001), and edited *Secret Spaces of Childhood* (University of Michigan Press 2003). A Fellow of the Society for Values in Higher Education, she is editor of the Landscapes of Childhood series at Wayne State University Press and an assistant editor of the *Michigan Quarterly Review*. A second book on play and a collection co-edited with Andrea Immel *Under Fire: Childhood in the Shadow of War* are forthcoming in 2008.